a Gift for:

_____

From:

_____

YOU CHANGED
MY LIFE BY:

_____
_____
_____
_____
_____
_____
_____

YOU
Changed My Life

MAX LUCADO

THOMAS NELSON
Since 1798

Hallmark
gift books

Cover photo-illustration: Rick Douglas
Interior images—p1(watering can): Image Copyright Alexander Raths, 2010 Used under license from Shutterstock.com
/ p14: Image Copyright Natalia D., 2010 Used under license from Shutterstock.com / p18: Image Copyright Kellie L.
Folkerts, 2010 Used under license from Shutterstock.com / p25: Image Copyright Steve Simzer, 2010 Used under license
from Shutterstock.com / p30: Image Copyright Shironina, 2010 Used under license from Shutterstock.com / p35: Image
Copyright John Wollwerth, 2010 Used under license from Shutterstock.com / p38: Image Copyright Khomulo Anna, 2010
Used under license from Shutterstock.com / p40: Image Copyright Ivan Cholakov Gostock-dot-net, 2010 Used under
license from Shutterstock.com / p43: Image Copyright Denis Tabler, 2010 Used under license from Shutterstock.com /
p50: Image Copyright Galushko Sergey, 2010 Used under license from Shutterstock.com / p58: Image Copyright Brent
Reeves, 2010 Used under license from Shutterstock.com / p66: Image Copyright Alex James Bramwell, 2010 Used under
license from Shutterstock.com / p70: Image Copyright Kapu, 2010 Used under license from Shutterstock.com / p81: Image
Copyright Sandra Cunningham, 2010 Used under license from Shutterstock.com / p87: Image Copyright Raia, 2010 Used
under license from Shutterstock.com / p90: Image Copyright jetsetmodels, 2010 Used under license from Shutterstock.
com / p103: Image Copyright JuliaSha, 2010 Used under license from Shutterstock.com / p111: Image Copyright Feng Yu,
2010 Used under license from Shutterstock.com / p117: Image Copyright Vaclav Volrab, 2010 Used under license from
Shutterstock.com / p125: Image Copyright Neal Digre, 2010 Used under license from Shutterstock.com / p131: Image
Copyright ATurner, 2010 Used under license from Shutterstock.com / p136: Image Copyright Jason E Day, 2010 Used
under license from Shutterstock.com / p152: Image Copyright Mikael Eriksson, 2010 Used under license from Shutterstock.
com / p157: Image Copyright Regien Paassen, 2010 Used under license from Shutterstock.com / p162: Image Copyright
emin kuliyev, 2010 Used under license from Shutterstock.com / p174: Image Copyright S. Hanusch, 2010 Used under
license from Shutterstock.com / p180: Image Copyright soMeth, 2010 Used under license from Shutterstock.com

ISBN: 978-1-59530-396-7
BOK3127

Printed and bound in China

Changed by

This book is for someone special. *You.*

"Who, me?" you're saying to yourself. Yes. You.

You made a difference in the life of the one who gave you this book. You shared words of wisdom, gave of yourself, mentored, led, walked alongside a hurting friend, took time to notice when others didn't. You did something for someone else. Your words, actions, time—whatever it was, you gave willingly, fully, selflessly. You changed a life.

And what you did mattered. Your actions mattered to the giver of this book. But more importantly, what you did mattered to the One who matters most. "God is fair; he will not forget the work you did and the love you showed for him by helping his people" (Hebrews 6:10 NCV).

May God's richest blessings be yours.

MAX LUCADO

⚜ 1 ⚜

CHANGED
BY LOVE

WHEN WE LOVE THOSE IN NEED,
WE ARE LOVING JESUS.

LOVE ON THE RIGHT SIDE

SHE CHOSE LOVE

LOVE MAKES A DIFFERENCE

CONFIDENT OF DAD'S LOVE

A REMARKABLE LOVE

HE SEES BEAUTY

I SEE LOVE AND UNSELFISHNESS

WHAT MADE HIM DO IT?

AGAPE LOVE

LOVE ON THE RIGHT SIDE

Over a hundred years ago in England, the borough of West Stanley endured a great tragedy. A mine collapsed, trapping and killing many of the workers inside. The

IT IS VERY DIFFICULT FOR US TO UNDERSTAND WHY GOD SHOULD LET SUCH AN AWFUL DISASTER HAPPEN, BUT WE KNOW HIM AND WE TRUST HIM, AND ALL WILL BE RIGHT.

bishop of Durham, Dr. Handley Moule, was asked to bring a word of comfort to the mourners. Standing at the mouth of the mine, he said, "It is very difficult for us to understand why God should let such an awful disaster happen, but we know Him and we trust Him, and all will be right. I have at home," he continued, "an old bookmark given to me by my mother. It is worked in silk, and, when I examine the wrong side of it, I see nothing but a tangle of threads, crossed and re-crossed. It looks like a big mistake. One would think that someone had done it who did not know what she was doing. But, when I turn it over and look at the right side, I see there, beautifully embroidered, the letters GOD IS LOVE.

"We are looking at this today," he counseled, "from the wrong side. Someday we shall see it from another standpoint, and shall understand." [1]

Every Day Deserves a Chance

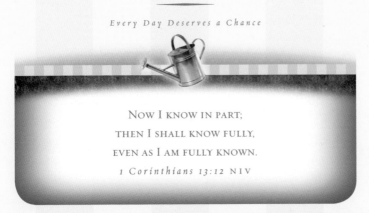

NOW I KNOW IN PART;
THEN I SHALL KNOW FULLY,
EVEN AS I AM FULLY KNOWN.
1 Corinthians 13:12 NIV

She Chose Love

Recently I shared a meal with some friends. A husband and wife wanted to tell me about a storm they were weathering. Through a series of events, she learned of an act of infidelity that had occurred over a decade ago.

WOULD THEY FLEE, FIGHT, OR FORGIVE?

He had made the mistake of thinking it'd be better not to tell her, so he didn't. But she found out. And as you can imagine, she was deeply hurt.

Through the advice of a counselor, the couple dropped everything and went away for several days. A decision had to be made. Would they flee, fight, or forgive? So they prayed. They talked. They walked. They reflected. In this case the wife was clearly in the right. She could have left. Women have done so for lesser reasons. Or she could have stayed and made his life a living hell. Other women have done that. But she chose a different response.

On the tenth night of their trip, my friend found a card on his pillow. On the card was a printed verse: "I'd rather do nothing with you than something without you." Beneath the verse she had written these words:

I forgive you. I love you. Let's move on.

Just Like Jesus

BE KIND TO ONE ANOTHER,
TENDERHEARTED, FORGIVING ONE ANOTHER,
EVEN AS GOD IN CHRIST FORGAVE YOU.
Ephesians 4:32

WANT TO SEE A MIRACLE? *Plant* A WORD OF LOVE
HEARTDEEP IN A PERSON'S LIFE. *Nurture* IT WITH
A SMILE AND A PRAYER, AND WATCH WHAT HAPPENS.

LOVE MAKES A DIFFERENCE

You know your love is real when you feel for others what Catherine Lawes felt for the inmates of Sing Sing prison. When her husband, Lewis, became the warden in 1921, she was a young mother of three daughters. Everybody warned her never to step foot inside the walls. But she didn't listen to them. When the first prison basketball game was held, in she went, three girls in tow, and took a seat in the bleachers with the inmates.

She once said, "My husband and I are going to take care of these men, and I believe they will take care of me! I don't have to worry!"

When she heard that one convicted murderer was blind, she taught him Braille so he could read. Upon learning of inmates who were hearing impaired, she studied sign language so they could communicate. For sixteen years Catherine Lawes softened the hard hearts of the men of Sing Sing. In 1937 the world saw the difference real love makes.

The prisoners knew something was wrong when Lewis Lawes didn't report to work. Quickly the word spread that Catherine had been killed in a car accident. The following day her body was placed in her home, three-quarters of a mile from the prison. As the acting warden

THESE WERE AMERICA'S HARDEST CRIMINALS. MURDERERS. ROBBERS. THESE WERE MEN THE NATION HAD LOCKED AWAY FOR LIFE.

took his early morning walk, he noticed a large gathering at the main gate. Every prisoner pressed against the fence. Eyes awash with tears. Faces solemn. No one spoke or moved. They'd come to stand as close as they could to the woman who'd given them love.

The warden made a remarkable decision. "All right, men, you can go. Just be sure to check in tonight." These were America's hardest criminals. Murderers. Robbers. These were men the nation had locked away for life. But the warden unlocked the gate for them, and they walked without escort or guard to the home of Catherine Lawes to pay their last respects. And to a man, each one returned. [2]

Real love changes people.

A Love Worth Giving

I WAS NAKED AND YOU CLOTHED ME; I WAS SICK
AND YOU VISITED ME; I WAS IN PRISON AND YOU
CAME TO ME. . . . ASSUREDLY, I SAY TO YOU, INASMUCH
AS YOU DID IT TO ONE OF THE LEAST OF THESE
MY BRETHREN, YOU DID IT TO ME.

Matthew 25:36, 40

Love LIKE THERE'S NO TOMORROW,
AND IF TOMORROW COMES, *love again*.

CONFIDENT OF DAD'S LOVE

Dropping a fly ball may not be a big deal to most people, but if you are thirteen years old and have aspirations of the big leagues, it is a big deal. Not only was it my second error of the game, it allowed the winning run to score.

I didn't even go back to the dugout. I turned around in the middle of left field and climbed over the fence. I was halfway home when my dad found me. He didn't say a word. Just pulled over to the side of the road, leaned across the seat, and opened the passenger door. We didn't speak. We didn't need to. We both knew the world had come to an end. When we got home, I went straight to my room, and he went straight to the kitchen. Presently he appeared in front of me with cookies and milk. He took a seat on the bed, and we broke bread together. Somewhere in the dunking of the cookies I began to realize that life and my father's love would go on. In the economy of male adolescence, if you love the guy who drops the ball, then you really love him. My skill as a baseball player didn't improve, but my confidence in Dad's love did. Dad never said a word. But he did show up. He did listen up.

A Love Worth Giving

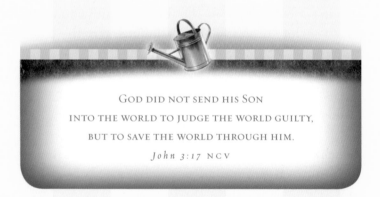

GOD DID NOT SEND HIS SON
INTO THE WORLD TO JUDGE THE WORLD GUILTY,
BUT TO SAVE THE WORLD THROUGH HIM.

John 3:17 NCV

A Remarkable Love

Dr. Maxwell Maltz tells a remarkable story of a love like this.

A man had been injured in a fire while attempting to save his parents from a burning house. He couldn't get to them. They perished. His face was burned and disfigured.

HER HUSBAND HAD REPEATEDLY REFUSED ANY HELP. SHE KNEW HE WOULD AGAIN.

He mistakenly interpreted his pain as God's punishment. The man wouldn't let anyone see him—not even his wife.

She went to Dr. Maltz, a plastic surgeon, for help. He told the woman not to worry. "I can restore his face."

The wife was unenthused. Her husband had repeatedly refused any help. She knew he would again.

Then why her visit? "I want you to disfigure my face so I can be like him! If I can share in his pain, then maybe he will let me back into his life."

Dr. Maltz was shocked. He denied her request but was so moved by this woman's love that he went to speak with her husband. Knocking on the man's bedroom door, he called loudly, "I'm a plastic surgeon, and I want you to know that I can restore your face."

No response.

"Please come out."

Again there was no answer.

Still speaking through the door, Dr. Maltz told the man of his wife's proposal. "She wants me to disfigure her face, to make her face like yours in the hope that you will let her back into your life. That's how much she loves you."

There was a brief moment of silence, and then, ever so slowly, the doorknob began to turn. [3]

Next Door Savior

SO THESE THREE THINGS
CONTINUE FOREVER: FAITH, HOPE, AND LOVE.
AND THE GREATEST OF THESE IS LOVE.
1 Corinthians 13:13 NCV

HE SEES BEAUTY

Years ago I met a woman who has experienced deep love.

Brain surgery has left her without the use of a facial nerve. As a result, she faces the world with a crooked smile. After the operation she met the love of her life. Here's how she describes him: "He sees nothing strange or ugly about me and has never, even in anger, made a joke about my appearance. He has never seen me any other way. When I look in the mirror, I see deformity, but my husband sees beauty."

Come Thirsty

A LITTLE *rain* CAN STRAIGHTEN A FLOWER STEM.

A LITTLE *love* CAN CHANGE A LIFE.

I See Love and Unselfishness

For the last five years my mother has been in an assisted-living facility not far from my house. The first few months I found it hard to see color amid the wrinkles, walkers, wheelchairs, and dentures. Each visit was a depressing reminder of my mom's failing health and fading memory.

Then I tried to practice the message of one of my books, *Give Every Day a Chance*, even the days of old age. I began to spot blades of grass amid the people.

The loyalty of Elaine, also eighty-seven, who sits next to Mom at lunch. She cuts my mother's food so she can eat it.

The unsquashable enthusiasm of Lois, nearly eighty, who in spite of arthritis in both knees volunteers to pour the morning coffee every day.

The historical love of Joe and Barbara, celebrating seventy years, not of life, but marriage. They take turns pushing each other in the wheelchair. Arthritis has enlarged the knuckles of her hand. We were no more than five minutes into the conversation, and he was gently lifting it toward me, expressing his concern.

Then there is Bob, left speechless and half-paralyzed by a stroke. The picture on his door displays a younger Bob, smartly attired in military uniform; he used to give orders and command troops. Today his good hand steers the joystick of his wheelchair as he goes from table to table wishing residents a good day by making the only sound he can: "Bmph."

I used to see age, disease, and faded vigor. Now I see love, courage, and unflappable unselfishness.

Every Day Deserves a Chance

WHAT MADE
HIM DO IT?

Jim Redmond's son Derek, a twenty-six-year-old Briton, was favored to win the four-hundred-meter race in the 1992 Barcelona Olympics. Halfway into his semifinal heat, a fiery pain seared through his right leg. He crumpled to the track with a torn hamstring.

As the medical attendants were approaching, Redmond fought to his feet. "It was animal instinct," he would later say. He set out hopping, pushing away the coaches in a crazed attempt to finish the race.

When he reached the stretch, a big man pushed through the crowd. He was wearing a t-shirt that read, "Have you hugged your child today?" and a hat that challenged, "Just Do It." The man was Jim Redmond, Derek's father.

"You don't have to do this," he told his weeping son.

"Yes, I do," Derek declared.

"Well, then," said Jim, "we're going to finish this together."

And they did. Jim wrapped Derek's arm around his shoulder and helped him hobble to the finish line. Fighting off security men, the son's head sometimes buried in the father's shoulder, they stayed in Derek's lane to the end.

The crowd clapped, then stood, then cheered, and then wept as the father and son finished the race.

What made the father do it? What made the father leave the stands to meet his son on the track? Was it the strength of his child? No, it was the pain of his child. His son was hurt and fighting to complete the race. So the father came to help him finish.

He Still Moves Stones

THE BEST TEST OF MY CHRISTIAN GROWTH

OCCURS IN THE *mainstream* OF LIFE,

NOT IN THE *quietness* OF MY STUDY.

AGAPE LOVE

I saw a shard of deep love between an elderly man and woman who have been married for fifty years. The last decade has been marred by her dementia. The husband did the best he could to care for his wife at home, but she grew sicker; he, older. So he admitted her to full-time care.

One day he asked me to visit her, so I did. Her room was spotless, thanks to his diligence. She, horizontal on the bed, was bathed and dressed, though going nowhere.

"I arrive at 6:15 a.m.," he beamed. "You'd think I was on the payroll. I feed her, bathe her, and stay with her. I will until one of us dies." Agape love.

3:16: The Numbers of Hope

2

Changed by Kindness

WORKS DONE IN GOD'S NAME
LONG OUTLIVE OUR EARTHLY LIVES.

KIND LIKE CHRIST

A GESTURE OF KINDNESS

KIND AND CONSIDERATE

A KISS OF KINDNESS

SMALL DEEDS MAKE BIG
DIFFERENCES

JAKE CARRIED THE BALL

A WORD OF AFFECTION

KIND LIKE CHRIST

A woman in a small Arkansas community was a single mom with a frail baby. Her neighbor would stop by every few days and keep the child so she could shop. After some weeks her neighbor shared more than time; she shared her faith, and the woman did what Matthew did. She followed Christ.

The friends of the young mother objected. "Do you know what those people teach?" they contested.

"Here is what I know," she told them. "They held my baby."[1]

Cast of Characters

I CHOOSE *kindness* . . .

I WILL BE KIND TO THE POOR, FOR THEY ARE ALONE.

KIND TO THE RICH, FOR THEY ARE AFRAID.

AND KIND TO THE UNKIND, FOR SUCH IS HOW *God* HAS TREATED ME.

A GESTURE OF KINDNESS

A friend of mine witnessed a humorous act of kindness at an auction. The purpose of the gathering was to raise money for a school. Someone had donated a purebred puppy that melted the heart and opened the checkbooks of many guests. Two in particular.

They sat on opposite sides of the banquet room, a man and a woman. As the bidding continued, these two surfaced as the most determined. Others dropped off, but not this duo. Back and forth they went until they'd one-upped the bid to several thousand dollars. This was no longer about a puppy. This was about victory. This was the Wimbledon finals, and neither player was backing off the net. (Don't you know the school president was drooling?)

Finally the fellow gave in and didn't return the bid. "Going once, going twice, going three times. Sold!" The place erupted, and the lady was presented with her tail-wagging trophy. Her face softened, then reddened. Maybe she'd forgotten where she was. Never intended to go twelve rounds at a formal dinner. Certainly never intended for the world to see her pit-bull side.

So you know what she did? As the applause subsided, she walked across the room and presented the puppy to the competition.

Suppose you did that with your competition. Suppose you surprised them with kindness? Not easy? No, it's not. But mercy is the deepest gesture of kindness.

A Love Worth Giving

Kindness IS CONTAGIOUS.

KIND AND
CONSIDERATE

Baron de Rothschild once asked artist Ary Scheffer to paint his portrait. Though a wealthy financier, Rothschild posed as a beggar, wearing rags and holding a tin cup. During one day of painting, a friend of the artist entered the room. Thinking Rothschild was really a beggar, he dropped a coin in his cup.

Ten years later that man received a letter from Baron de Rothschild and a check for ten thousand francs. The message read, "You one day gave a coin to Baron de Rothschild in the studio of Ary Scheffer. He has invested it and today sends you the capital which you entrusted to him, together with the compounded interest. A good action always brings good fortune." [3]

Cure for the Common Life

KIND HEARTS ARE *quietly kind.* THEY LET THE CAR CUT INTO TRAFFIC AND THE YOUNG MOM WITH THREE KIDS MOVE UP IN THE CHECKOUT LINE. THEY PICK UP THE NEIGHBOR'S TRASHCAN THAT ROLLED INTO THE STREET.

A KISS OF
KINDNESS

I received a call from a friend named Kenny. He and his family had just returned from Disney World. "I saw a sight I'll never forget," he said. "I want you to know about it."

He and his family were inside Cinderella's castle. It was packed with kids and parents. Suddenly all the children rushed to one side. Had it been a boat, the castle would have tipped over. Cinderella had entered.

Cinderella. The pristine princess. Kenny said she was perfectly typecast. A gorgeous young girl with each hair in place, flawless skin, and a beaming smile. She stood waist-deep in a garden of kids, each wanting to touch and be touched.

For some reason Kenny turned and looked toward the other side of the castle. It was now vacant except for a boy maybe seven or eight years old. His age was hard to determine because of the disfigurement of his body. Dwarfed in height, face deformed, he stood watching quietly and wistfully, holding the hand of an older brother.

Don't you know what he wanted? He wanted to be with the children. He longed to be in the middle of the kids reaching for Cinderella, calling her name. But can't you feel his fear, fear of yet another rejection? Fear of being taunted again, mocked again?

Don't you wish Cinderella would go to him? Guess what? She did!

She noticed the little boy. She immediately began walking in his direction. Politely but firmly inching through the crowd of children, she finally broke free. She walked quickly across the floor, knelt at eye level with the stunned little boy, and placed a kiss on his face.

A Gentle Thunder

Kindness NOT ONLY MAKES THE COFFEE.

KINDNESS SAYS *good morning*.

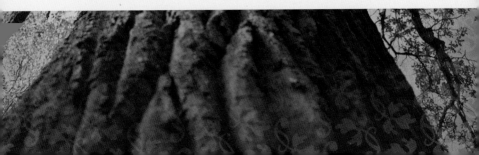

SMALL DEEDS MAKE BIG DIFFERENCES

World War II had decimated Germany. Citizens clamored for supplies. Russia reduced Berlin's buildings to skeletons and sought to do the same to her people. They blockaded food-bearing trucks, trains, and boats. Without help, the city would starve. The U.S. and British military responded with the 1948 airlift. For eleven months, they airdropped tons of food to the 2.5 million Berliners.

Gail Halvorsen piloted one of the planes for the United States. After landing in Berlin one day, the twenty-seven-year-old talked with thirty or so German children through a barbed-wire fence. Though hungry and needy, they didn't beg or complain.

Impressed, Halvorsen reached into his pocket, produced two sticks of gum, broke them in half, and handed the pieces through the wire. "Those kids looked like they had just received a million bucks," he recounted. "They put that tiny piece of paper to their noses and smelled the aroma. They were on cloud nine. I stood there dumbfounded."

Touched by their plight, Halvorsen promised to return the next day and drop more gum from his plane. With

---

THOUGH HUNGRY AND NEEDY,
THEY DIDN'T BEG OR COMPLAIN.

---

supply flights landing every half-hour, the children asked how they'd recognize him. "I'll wiggle my wings," he replied.

Halvorsen returned to Rhein-Main Air Force Base and bought gum and candy rations from his buddies. He tied the sweets to tiny handkerchief parachutes, loaded them on his C-54, and, true to his word, wiggled his wings over

Berlin. Kids in the city streets spotted their friend and ran to gather the falling candy.

Operation Little Vittles had begun. Momentum mounted quickly. Within three weeks the Air Force sanctioned the crusade. During the following months, U.S. planes dropped three tons of candy on the city. The pilot became known as Uncle Wiggly Wings. [4]

Cure for the Common Life

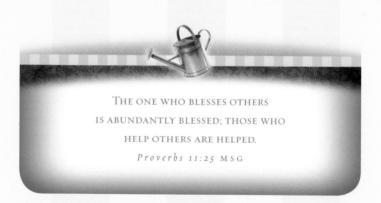

THE ONE WHO BLESSES OTHERS
IS ABUNDANTLY BLESSED; THOSE WHO
HELP OTHERS ARE HELPED.
Proverbs 11:25 M S G

Jake Carried the Ball

When seventeen-year-old Jake Porter ran onto the football field, both teams cheered. Odd that they would. In three years on the Northwest High squad, he'd barely

THE MCDERMOTT, OHIO, FANS HAD NEVER SEEN JAKE CARRY THE BALL OR MAKE A TACKLE.

dirtied a game jersey. The McDermott, Ohio, fans had never seen Jake carry the ball or make a tackle. Nor had they seen him read a book or write much more than a sentence. Kids with chromosomal fragile X syndrome, a common cause of mental retardation, seldom do.

But Jake loved sports. Each day after his special-ed classes, he dashed off to some practice: track, baseball, basketball. Never missed. Never played, either.

Until the Waverly game.

Jake's coach made his decision before the kickoff. If a lop-sided score rendered the final seconds superfluous, Jake would come in. The lopsided part proved true. With five ticks remaining on the clock, his team was down 42–0. So the coach called a time-out.

He motioned to speak with the opposing coach. As his Waverly counterpart heard the plan, he began shaking his head and waving his hands. He disagreed with some-thing. A referee intervened, and play resumed.

The quarterback took the ball and handed it to Jake. Jake knew what do: take a knee and let the clock expire. They'd practiced this play all week. But, to his surprise, the players wouldn't let him. His teammates told him to run. So he did. In the wrong direction. So the back judge stopped and turned him around.

That's when the Waverly defense did their part. The vis-iting coach, as it turns out, wasn't objecting to the play.

He was happy for Porter to carry the ball, but not for him just to run out the clock. He wanted Jake to score. Waverly players parted like the Red Sea for Moses and shouted for Jake to run. Run he did. Grinning and dancing and jumping all the way to the end zone.

Both sidelines celebrated. Moms cried, cheerleaders whooped, and Jake smiled as if he'd won the lottery without buying a ticket. [5]

Come Thirsty

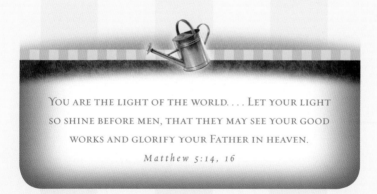

YOU ARE THE LIGHT OF THE WORLD. . . . LET YOUR LIGHT SO SHINE BEFORE MEN, THAT THEY MAY SEE YOUR GOOD WORKS AND GLORIFY YOUR FATHER IN HEAVEN.

Matthew 5:14, 16

WHEN YOU GIVE A WORD OF *kindness* TO SOMEONE
WHO NEEDS IT, THAT'S AN ACT OF *worship*.

A WORD OF AFFECTION

Leo Tolstoy, the great Russian writer, tells of the time he was walking down the street and passed a beggar. Tolstoy reached into his pocket to give the beggar some money, but his pocket was empty. Tolstoy turned to the man and said, "I'm sorry, my brother, but I have nothing to give."

The beggar brightened and said, "You have given me more than I asked for—you have called me brother."

To the loved, a word of affection is a morsel, but to the love-starved, a word of affection can be a feast.

He Still Moves Stones

3

CHANGED BY COMMITMENT

GOD CHANGES THE WORLD
WITH FOLKS LIKE YOU AND ME.

A DAD WHO DIDN'T QUIT

RESCUED

UNWAVERING COMMITMENT

MAKING A DIFFERENCE

PRODIGAL PATH

THE STRONG SPEAKING FOR
THE WEAK

LET'S MAKE IT TO THE TOP

A Dad Who Didn't Quit

The 1989 Armenian earthquake needed only four minutes to flatten the nation and kill thirty thousand people. Moments after the deadly tremor ceased, a father raced to an elementary school to save his son. When he arrived, he saw that the building had been leveled. Looking at the mass of stones and rubble, he remembered a promise he had made to his child: "No matter what happens, I'll always be there for you." Driven by his own promise, he found the area closest to his son's room and began to pull back the rocks. Other parents arrived and began sobbing for their children. "It's too late," they told the man. "You know they are dead. You can't help." Even a police officer encouraged him to give up.

But the father refused. For eight hours, then sixteen, then thirty-two, thirty-six hours he dug. His hands were raw and his energy gone, but he refused to quit. Finally, after thirty-eight wrenching hours, he pulled back a boulder and heard his son's voice. He called his boy's name, "Arman! Arman!" And a voice answered him, "Dad, it's me!" Then the boy added these priceless words, "I told the other kids not to worry. I told them if you were alive, you'd save me, and when you saved me, they'd be saved too. Because you promised, 'No matter what, I'll always be there for you.'" [1]

When Christ Comes

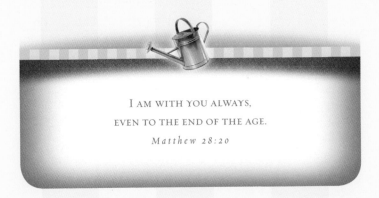

I AM WITH YOU ALWAYS,
EVEN TO THE END OF THE AGE.

Matthew 28:20

RESCUED

Ernstena is a pastor's wife. Clara is a businesswoman. Jo Anne had just started a small relief organization. They traveled to Cambodia to encourage Jim-Lo, a missionary friend. He led them to a section of his city where the modern sex trade runs rampant. An estimated fifteen thousand girls were on sale. At the time more than a hundred thousand young women in Cambodia had been sold into forced prostitution. Jo Anne, Clara, Ernstena, and Jim-Lo looked into the faces of teen girls, even preteens, and could see a devastating story in each. They began to snap pictures until the sellers threatened to take the camera away. The Christians had no idea what to do but pray.

The seedy avenue became their Upper Room. *Lord, what do you want us to do? It's so overwhelming.* They wept.

God heard their prayer and gave them their tools. Upon

returning to the United States, Jo Anne wrote an article about the experience, which prompted a reader to send a good deal of money. With this gift the women formed an anti-trafficking ministry of World Hope International and provided housing for the young girls who were rescued or escaped from the brothels and sales stations. In just three years, four hundred children, ranging in age from two to fifteen, were rescued.

When the U.S. State Department sponsored an event called "The Salute to the 21st Century Abolitionists," they honored World Hope. They even asked one of the women to offer a prayer. The prayer that began on a Cambodian street continued in front of some of the most influential government officials in the world. [2]

SPEAK WORDS THAT MAKE PEOPLE *stronger*.
BELIEVE IN THEM AS *God* HAS BELIEVED IN YOU.

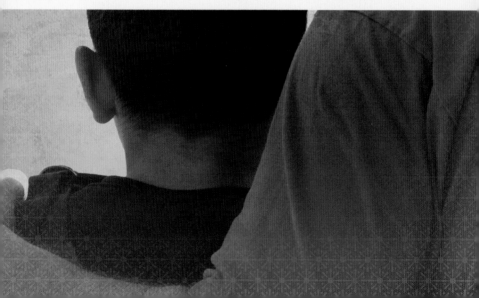

Unwavering Commitment

It was a long summer. I was thirteen, a left-fielder on the local Pony League team. I held the record for the most strikeouts . . . as a batter, not as a pitcher. I went the entire season and got only two hits. Over sixty times at bat and only two hits.

Two hits! That's not even good enough to be called a slump! That's a lot of long walks from the plate to the dugout. It got to the point that my team moaned when my time at bat was called. (The other team cheered.) Pretty tough on the self-image of a thirteen-year-old who had dreams of playing for the Dodgers.

The only thing right that summer was my parents' attitude toward my "slump." They never missed a game. Never. Not once did I look up and see their bleacher seats unoccupied. I was still their boy even if I led the league in strikeouts. Their commitment ran deeper than my performance. They showed me the importance of unwavering commitment.

On the Anvil

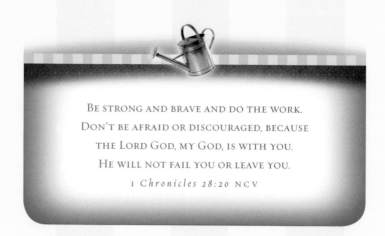

BE STRONG AND BRAVE AND DO THE WORK.
DON'T BE AFRAID OR DISCOURAGED, BECAUSE
THE LORD GOD, MY GOD, IS WITH YOU.
HE WILL NOT FAIL YOU OR LEAVE YOU.

1 Chronicles 28:20 NCV

MAKING A
DIFFERENCE

I have a friend who teaches at a public elementary school. By God's description she pastors a class of precious children. Read the e-mail she sent her friends:

> I'm asking for your prayers for my students. I know everyone is busy, but if you ever can, I know there is power in specifically addressed prayers.

I KNOW THERE IS POWER IN SPECIFICALLY ADDRESSED PRAYERS.

Please pray for . . .

Randy (smartest boy in my class—mom speaks no English—just moved from Washington—blind in his right eye because he poked his eye with a sharp tool when he was three.)

Henry (learning disabled—tries with all his little heart—it takes him about a minute to say two words—I think he's used to me now, but it was hard for him to keep up at first!)

Richard (a smile that could almost get him out of any trouble—his mom can't be much older than I am—he's very smart and pretty naughty, just the way I like 'em!)

Anna (learning disability—neither parent can read, write, or drive—they have four children!!! who knows how they keep it together—colors me a picture every single day, writes her spelling sentences about me, I'm the main character in her stories.)

On and on the list goes, including nearly deaf Sara. Dis-organized-but-thoughtful Terrell. Model-student Alicia. Bossy-but-creative Kaelyn.

Does this teacher work for a school system or for God? Does she spend her day in work or worship? Does she make money or a difference?

Cure for the Common Life

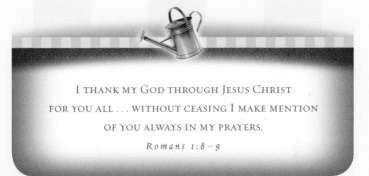

I THANK MY GOD THROUGH JESUS CHRIST
FOR YOU ALL . . . WITHOUT CEASING I MAKE MENTION
OF YOU ALWAYS IN MY PRAYERS.

Romans 1:8 – 9

PRODIGAL PATH

When I was seven years old, I ran away from home. I'd had enough of my father's rules and decided I could make it on my own, thank you very much. With my clothes in a paper bag, I stormed out the back gate and marched down the alley. Like the prodigal son, I decided I needed no father. Unlike the prodigal son, I didn't go far. I got to the end of the alley and remembered I was hungry, so I went back home.

But though the rebellion was brief, it was rebellion nonetheless. And had you stopped me on that prodigal path between the fences and asked me who my father was, I just might have told you how I felt. I just might have said, "I don't need a father. I'm too big for the rules of my family. It's just me, myself, and my paper bag." I don't remember saying that to anyone, but I remember thinking it. And I also remember rather sheepishly stepping in the back door and taking my seat at the supper table across from the very father I had, only moments before, disowned.

Did he know of my insurrection? I suspect he did. Did he know of my denial? Dads usually do. Was I still his son? Apparently so. (No one else was sitting in my place.) Had you gone to my father after you had spoken to me and asked, "Mr. Lucado, your son says he has no need of a father. Do you still consider him your son?" what would my dad have said?

I don't have to guess at his answer. He called himself my father even when I didn't call myself his son. His commitment to me was greater than my commitment to him.

The Great House of God

GOD LOVES ME AND MAKES ME HIS *child.*

God LOVES MY NEIGHBOR

AND MAKES HIM MY *brother.*

THE STRONG
SPEAKING FOR
THE WEAK

I witnessed a picture of the strong speaking for the weak during a White House briefing on the AIDS crisis. While most of the attendees represented relief organizations, a few ministers were invited. The agenda of the day included a Q and A with a White House staffer charged with partial oversight of several billion dollars earmarked for AIDS prevention and treatment. There were many questions. How does one qualify? How much can an organization hope to receive? What are the requirements, if any, for using the moneys? Most of the questions came from organizations. Most of us ministers were silent.

But not Bob Coy. Bob serves a large congregation in Fort Lauderdale, Florida. From earlier conversations, I knew of his heart for AIDS victims. When he raised his hand, I expected a policy question. Wrong. He had a personal question. "One of my friends in Miami is dying from AIDS. He spends two thousand dollars a month on medication. With insurance balking at coverage, I'm wondering if I might find him some assistance."

The White House policy staffer was surprised, but polite. "Uh, sure. After the meeting I'll put you in touch with the right person."

The minister, determined to bring the problem to the top of the food chain, remained standing. He held up a few sheets of stapled paper. "I brought his documents with me. If more is needed, I can run them down."

The government official remained polite. "Absolutely. After the meeting."

He had fielded another question or two when he noticed the minister from Florida had raised his hand again.

This time the preacher went to the bottom line. "I'm still thinking of my friend," he explained. "Who signs the checks?"

"Excuse me?"

"Who signs the checks? I just want to talk to the person who makes the decisions. So I want to know, who signs the checks?"

My initial response was, *What audacity!* The minister seizing a White House moment to help a friend. Then I thought, *What loyalty!* Does the bedridden friend in Florida have any idea that his cause is being presented a few hundred feet from the Oval Office?

The AIDS-infected man has no voice, no clout, and no influence. But he has a friend. And his friend speaks on his behalf.

Come Thirsty

WHEN WE DO *good* THINGS TO OTHERS

WE DO GOOD THINGS TO *God*.

Let's Make It to the Top

The view from Colorado's Mount Chrysolite steals what little breath the climb doesn't. A shawl of snow rests on the peaks to the east, marking the Continental Divide. You'd swear that's Montana you see to the north. Circles of ice-cold, trout-packed, pristine ponds stretch through the valley beneath you like a straight string of pearls.

Each Thursday during the summer, some four hundred kids make the fourteen-thousand-foot climb. They've traveled from all over the nation to spend a week at Frontier Ranch, a Young Life camp. Some come to escape parents or hang out with a boyfriend. But before the week culminates, all hear about Jesus. And all will witness his work from the top of Mount Chrysolite.

They all will climb the peak. For that reason, several Young Life directors caboose the end of the pack. They prod and applaud, making sure every camper crests the top. I walked with them.

One young student, whose sweet spot shows great actuarial potential, counted the strides to the peak. Eight thousand. Somewhere around number four thousand Matthew from Minnesota decided to call it quits, said he was too tired to take another step. [3]

I took a quick liking to the guy. Most anyone would. Jovial. Pleasant and, in this case, donkey-determined not to climb that mountain. He let everyone but a few of us pass him. "I'm heading down," he announced. A Young Life staffer spelled out the consequences. "Can't send you down alone, friend. You turn back, we all turn back."

The small circle of "we" I realized included "me." I didn't want to go back. I had two options: miss the mountaintop or help Matt see it.

I coaxed him, begged him, negotiated a plan with him. Thirty steps of walking. Sixty seconds of resting. We inched our way at this pace for an hour. Finally we stood within a thousand feet of the peak. But the last stretch of trail rose up as straight as a fireman's ladder.

We got serious. Two guys each took an arm, and I took the rear. I placed both hands on Matt's gluteus maximus and shoved. We all but drug him past the timberline.

That's when we heard the applause. Four hundred kids on the crest of Mount Chrysolite gave Matt from Minnesota a standing ovation. They whooped and hollered and slapped him on the back.

As I slumped down to rest, this thought steamrolled my way: *There it is, Max, a picture of my plan. Do all you can to push each other to the top.*

Cure for the Common Life

4

CHANGED
BY COMPASSION

WE ARE CREATED BY A
GREAT GOD TO DO GREAT WORKS.

SAVE ONE LIFE, SAVE THE WORLD

PEOPLE AREN'T PROBLEMS,
THEY'RE OPPORTUNITIES

HE SAW DEEP WITHIN

RECKLESS LOVERS OF LIFE

MY FATHER, MY FRIEND

SECOND-MILE COMPASSION

HE STOLE MY HEART

SAVE ONE LIFE,
SAVE THE WORLD

Twenty-two people traveled to London on a fall morning in 2009 to thank Nicholas Winton. They could have passed for a retirement home social club. All were in their seventies and eighties. . . .

But this was no social trip. It was a journey of gratitude. They came to thank the man who saved their lives: a stooped centenarian who met them on this train platform just as he did in 1939.

He was a twenty-nine-year-old stockbroker at the time. Hitler's armies were ravaging the nation of Czechoslovakia, tearing Jewish families apart, and marching parents to concentration camps. No one was caring for the children.

Winton got wind of their plight and resolved to help them. He used his vacation to travel to Prague where he met the parents who, incredibly, were willing to entrust their children's future to his care. Returning to England, he worked his regular job on the Stock Exchange by day and advocated for the children at night. He convinced

THEY CAME TO THANK THE MAN WHO SAVED THEIR LIVES: A STOOPED CENTENARIAN WHO MET THEM ON THIS TRAIN PLATFORM JUST AS HE DID IN 1939.

Great Britain to permit their entry. He found foster homes and raised funds. He scheduled his first transport on March 14, 1939, and accomplished seven more over the next five months. His last trainload of children arrived on August 2, bringing the total of rescued children to 669.

On September 1, the biggest transport was to take place, but Hitler invaded Poland and Germany, closing borders throughout Europe. None of the 250 children on that train were ever seen again.

After the war, Winton didn't tell anyone of his rescue efforts, even his wife. In 1988, she found a scrapbook in their attic, with all the children's photos and a complete list of names. She prodded him to tell the story. As he has, rescued children have returned to say thank you. The grateful group includes a film director, a Canadian journalist, a news correspondent, a former minister in the British Cabinet, a magazine manager, and one of the founders of the Israeli Air Force. There are some 7,000 children, grandchildren, and great-grandchildren who owe their ancestry to Winton's bravery. He wears a ring given to him by some of the children he saved. It bears a line from the Talmud, the book of Jewish law. "Save one life. Save the world." [1]

Outlive Your Life

PEOPLE AREN'T PROBLEMS, THEY'RE OPPORTUNITIES

My friend Roosevelt is a leader in our congregation and one of the nicest guys in the history of humanity. He lives next door to a single mom who was cited by their homeowner's association for an unkempt lawn. A jungle of overgrown bushes and untrimmed trees obscured her house. The association warned her to get her yard cleaned up. It was a blight on the street, maybe even a health hazard.

Roosevelt, however, paid his neighbor, Terry, a visit. There is always a story behind the door, and he found a sad one. She had just weathered a rough divorce, was undergoing chemotherapy, working a night shift at the hospital and extra hours to make ends meet. She was in survival mode: alone, sick, and exhausted. Lawn care? The least of her concerns.

So Roosevelt recruited several neighbors, and the families spent a Saturday morning getting things in order. They cut shrubs and branches and carted out a dozen bags of leaves. A few days later Terry sent this message to the board of the homeowners association:

> Dear Sirs,
> I am hoping that you can let the neighborhood be aware of a great group of neighbors I have....
>
> Their actions encouraged me to realize that there are still some compassionate people residing here. . . . These residents are to be commended, and I cannot adequately express how grateful I am for their hard work, positive attitude, and enthusiasm. Thank you!

Roosevelt's response was a Christ-like response. Rather than see people as problems, Christ saw them as opportunities.

LIVE IN SUCH A WAY

THAT THE WORLD WILL BE *glad* YOU DID.

HE SAW DEEP WITHIN

Stanley Shipp served as a father to my young faith. He was thirty years my senior and blessed with a hawkish nose, thin lips, a rim of white hair, and a heart as big as the Midwest. His business cards, which he gave to those who requested and those who didn't, read simply, "Stanley Shipp—Your Servant."

I spent my first postcollege year under his tutelage. One of our trips took us to a small church in rural Pennsylvania for a conference. He and I happened to be the only two people at the building when a drifter, wearing alcohol like a cheap perfume, knocked on the door. He recited his victim spiel. Overqualified for work. Unqualified for pension. Lost bus ticket. Bad back. His kids in Kansas didn't care. If bad breaks were rock and roll, this guy was Elvis. I crossed my arms, smirked, and gave Stanley a get-a-load-of-this-guy glance.

Stanley didn't return it. He devoted every optic nerve to the drifter.

Stanley saw no one else but him. *How long,* I remember wondering, *since anyone looked this fellow square in the face?*

The meandering saga finally stopped, and Stanley led the man into the church kitchen and prepared him a plate of food and a sack of groceries.

As we watched him leave, Stanley blinked back a tear and responded to my unsaid thoughts. "Max, I know he's probably lying. But what if just one part of his story was true?"

We both saw the man. I saw right through him. Stanley saw deep into him. There is something fundamentally good about taking time to see a person.

Outlive Your Life

RECKLESS LOVERS OF LIFE

Here's to the hero of the San Francisco marathon who crossed the finish line without seeing it. (He was blind.)

Here's to the woman whose husband left her with a nest of kids to raise and bills to pay, but who somehow tells me every Sunday that God has never been closer.

Here's to the single father of two girls who learned to braid their hair.

Here's to the grandparents who came out of retirement to raise the children their children couldn't raise.

Here's to the foster parents who took in a child long enough for that child to take their hearts—then gave the child up again.

Here's to the girl, told by everyone to abort the baby, who chose to keep the baby.

Here's to the doctor who treats more than half of his patients for free.

Here's to the heroin-addict-turned-missionary.

Here's to the executive who every Tuesday hosts a 5:30 a.m. meeting for Bible study and prayer.

Here's to all of you reckless lovers of life and God.

In the Eye of the Storm

My Father, My Friend

I know a father who, out of love for his son, spends each night in a recliner, never sleeping more than a couple of consecutive hours. A car accident paralyzed the teenager. To maintain the boy's circulation, therapists massage his limbs every few hours. At night the father takes the place of the therapists. Though he's worked all day and will work again the next, he sets the alarm to wake himself every other hour until sunrise.

3:16: The Numbers of Hope

GOD USES PEOPLE TO CHANGE THE WORLD. *People!* NOT SAINTS OR SUPERHUMANS.

SECOND-MILE COMPASSION

Let's talk about the Society of the Second Mile.

A second-miler serves in our children's ministry. She creates crafts and take-home gifts for four-year-olds. Completing the craft is not enough, however. She has to give it a second-mile touch. When a class followed the theme "Walking in the Steps of Jesus," she made cookies in the shape of a foot and, in second-mile fashion, painted a toenail on each cookie. Who does that?

Second-milers do. They clean bathrooms, decorate cookies, and build playrooms in their houses. At least Bob and Elsie did. They built an indoor pool, bought a Ping-Pong table and foosball game. They created a kid's paradise.

Not unusual, you say? Oh, I forgot to mention their age. They did this in their seventies. They did this because they loved the lonely youth of downtown Miami. Bob didn't swim. Elsie didn't play Ping-Pong. But the kids of immigrant Cubans did. And Bob could be seen each week driving his Cadillac through Little Havana, picking up the teens other people forgot.

The Society of the Second Mile. Let me tell you how to spot its members. They don't wear badges or uniforms; they wear smiles. They have discovered the secret. The joy is found in the extra effort.

They've discovered this truth: "Self-help is no help at all. Self-sacrifice is the way, my way, to finding yourself, your true self" (Luke 9:24 MSG).

Every Day Deserves a Chance

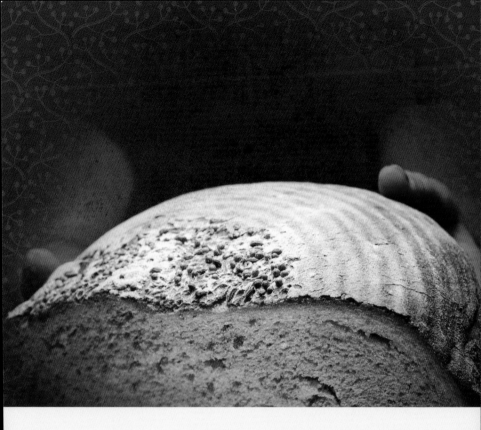

NONE OF US CAN HELP *everyone*.

BUT ALL OF US CAN HELP *someone*.

He Stole
My Heart

He couldn't have been over six years old. Dirty face, bare-footed, torn T-shirt, matted hair. He wasn't too different from the other hundred thousand or so street orphans that roam Rio de Janeiro.

I was walking to get a cup of coffee at a nearby cafe when he came up behind me. With my thoughts somewhere between the task I had just finished and the class I was about to teach, I scarcely felt the tap, tap, tap on my hand. I stopped and turned. Seeing no one, I continued on my way. I'd only taken a few steps, however, when I felt another insistent tap, tap, tap. This time I stopped and looked downward. There he stood. His eyes were whiter because of his grubby cheeks and coal-black hair.

"Pão, senhor?" ("Bread, sir?")

Living in Brazil, one has daily opportunities to buy a candy bar or sandwich for these little outcasts. It's the least one can do. I told him to come with me and we entered the sidewalk cafe. "Coffee for me and something tasty for my little friend." The boy ran to the pastry coun-

NORMALLY, THESE YOUNGSTERS TAKE THE FOOD AND SCAMPER BACK OUT INTO THE STREET WITHOUT A WORD.

ter and made his choice. Normally, these youngsters take the food and scamper back out into the street without a word. But this little fellow surprised me.

The cafe consisted of a long bar: one end for pastries and the other for coffee. As the boy was making his choice, I went to the other end of the bar and began drinking my coffee. Just as I was getting my derailed train of thought back on track, I saw him again. He was standing in the cafe entrance, on tiptoe, bread in hand, looking in at the people. *What's he doing?* I thought.

Then he saw me and scurried in my direction. He came and stood in front of me about eye-level with my belt buckle. The little Brazilian orphan looked up at the big American missionary, smiled a smile that would have stolen your heart and said, "Obrigado." (Thank you.) Then, nervously scratching the back of his ankle with his big toe, he added, "Muito obrigado." (Thank you very much.)

All of a sudden, I had a crazy craving to buy him the whole restaurant.

No Wonder They Call Him the Savior

LET THE LITTLE CHILDREN COME TO ME,
AND DO NOT HINDER THEM, FOR THE KINGDOM
OF GOD BELONGS TO SUCH AS THESE.

Mark 10:14

❈ 5 ❈

CHANGED
BY HOPE

NO ONE CAN DO EVERYTHING,
BUT EVERYONE CAN DO SOMETHING.

HOPE-FILLED WORDS

DAD LEARNED HIS LANGUAGE

A SERMON OF HOPE

BELIEVING WHAT HE HOPED

THE GIFT OF HOPE

"JUST WONDERFUL!"

A MISSION OF MERCY AND HOPE

YOU ARE SPECIAL

HOPE-FILLED WORDS

Nathaniel Hawthorne came home heartbroken. He'd just been fired from his job in the custom house. His wife, rather than responding with anxiety, surprised him with joy.

"Now you can write your book!"

He wasn't so positive. "And what shall we live on while I'm writing it?"

To his amazement she opened a drawer and revealed a wad of money she'd saved out of her housekeeping budget. "I always knew you were a man of genius," she told him. "I always knew you'd write a masterpiece."

She believed in her husband. And because she did, he
wrote. And because he wrote, every library in America
has a copy of *The Scarlet Letter* by Nathaniel Hawthorne. [1]

A Love Worth Giving

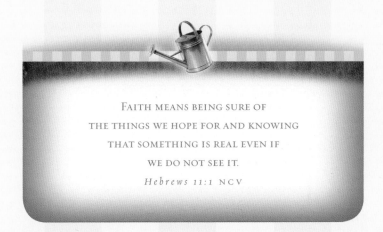

FAITH MEANS BEING SURE OF
THE THINGS WE HOPE FOR AND KNOWING
THAT SOMETHING IS REAL EVEN IF
WE DO NOT SEE IT.
Hebrews 11:1 NCV

DAD LEARNED
HIS LANGUAGE

My Uncle Carl was grateful that someone spoke to him. A childhood case of the measles left him unable to hear or speak. Nearly all of his sixty-plus years were lived in stony silence. Few people spoke his language.

My father was one of them. Being the older brother, maybe he felt protective. After their father died, perhaps

> LET DAD ENTER THE ROOM, AND
> CARL'S FACE WOULD BRIGHTEN.

he felt he should take over. Whatever the reason, my dad learned sign language. Dad wasn't an avid student. He never finished high school. Never went to college. Never saw the need to learn Spanish or French. But he did take the time to learn the language of his brother.

Let Dad enter the room, and Carl's face would brighten. The two would find a corner, and the hands would fly, and they would have a great time. And though I never heard Carl say thanks (he couldn't), his huge smile left no doubt that he was grateful. My dad had learned his language.

He Chose the Nails

HOW SWEET ARE YOUR WORDS TO MY TASTE,
SWEETER THAN HONEY TO MY MOUTH.

Psalm 119:103

A Sermon
of Hope

John Egglen had never preached a sermon in his life.
Never.

Wasn't that he didn't want to, just never needed to. But
then one morning he did. The snow left his town of Col-
chester, England, buried in white. When he awoke on
that January Sunday in 1850, he thought of staying home.
Who would go to church in such weather?

But he reconsidered. He was, after all, a deacon. And if
the deacons didn't go, who would? So he put on his boots,
hat, and coat and walked the six miles to the Methodist
Church.

He wasn't the only member who considered staying
home. In fact, he was one of the few who came. Only

thirteen people were present. Twelve members and one visitor. Even the minister was snowed in. Someone suggested they go home. Egglen would hear none of that. They'd come this far; they would have a service. Besides, they had a visitor. A thirteen-year-old boy.

But who would preach? Egglen was the only deacon. It fell to him.

And so he did. His sermon lasted only ten minutes. It drifted and wandered and made no point in an effort to make several. But at the end, an uncharacteristic cour-

WHO WOULD GO TO CHURCH IN SUCH WEATHER?

age settled upon the man. He lifted his eyes and looked straight at the boy and challenged: "Young man, look to Jesus. Look! Look! Look!"

Did the challenge make a difference? Let the boy, now a man, answer. "I did look, and then and there the cloud on my heart lifted, the darkness rolled away, and at that moment I saw the sun."

The boy's name? Charles Haddon Spurgeon. England's prince of preachers. [2]

Did Egglen know what he'd done? No.

Do heroes know when they are heroic? Rarely.

Cast of Characters

THE WORDS THAT I SPEAK
TO YOU ARE SPIRIT, AND THEY ARE LIFE.

John 6:63

PEOPLE WILL *know* WE ARE CHRISTIANS,

NOT BECAUSE WE BEAR THE *name*,

BUT BECAUSE WE *live* THE LIFE.

BELIEVING WHAT
HE HOPED

In the book *Life Verses*, Frank Boreham tells the story of a British minister by the name of Bernard Gilpin who, under Queen Mary, was sentenced to die for his faith. During his imprisonment he cast all his hope on the truth of Romans 8:28. He quoted the verse throughout the day, "We know that in everything God works for the good of those who love him" NCV.

On his way to execution he fell and broke his leg. He was ordered back to prison and, while moaning in pain, the jailer mocked his trust in this text. "Ah," Gilpin replied, "It's true all the same. It's all working together for good." And surely enough, it was. While he recovered, Mary died and Bernard Gilpin was released. God is working for the good of his children and he is using everything to accomplish it.

From Max's sermon titled, "Wait 3"

LET US HOLD FAST
THE CONFESSION OF OUR HOPE
WITHOUT WAVERING,
FOR HE WHO PROMISED IS FAITHFUL.

Hebrews 10:23

THE GIFT
OF HOPE

The aspiring young author was in need of hope. More than one person had told him to give up. "Getting published is impossible," one mentor said. "Unless you are a national celebrity, publishers won't talk to you." Another warned, "Writing takes too much time. Besides, you don't want all your thoughts on paper."

Initially he listened. He agreed that writing was a waste of effort and turned his attention to other projects. But somehow the pen and pad were bourbon and Coke to the wordaholic. He'd rather write than read. So he wrote. How many nights did he pass on that couch in the corner of the apartment reshuffling his deck of verbs and nouns? And how many hours did his wife sit with him? He word-smithing. She cross-stitching. Finally a manuscript was finished. Crude and laden with mistakes but finished.

She gave him the shove. "Send it out. What's the harm?"

So out it went. Mailed to fifteen different publishers. While the couple waited, he wrote. While he wrote, she stitched. Neither expecting much, both hoping every-

---

I'M SORRY, BUT WE DON'T ACCEPT UNSOLICITED MANUSCRIPTS.

---

thing. Responses began to fill the mailbox. "I'm sorry, but we don't accept unsolicited manuscripts." "We must return your work. Best of luck." "Our catalog doesn't have room for unpublished authors."

I still have those letters. Somewhere in a file. Finding them would take some time. Finding Denalyn's cross-stitch, however, would take none. To see it, all I do is lift my eyes from this monitor and look on the wall: Of all those arts in which the wise excel, nature's chief masterpiece is writing well.

She gave it to me about the time the fifteenth letter arrived. A publisher had said yes. That letter is also framed. Which of the two is more meaningful? The gift from my wife or the letter from the publisher? The gift, hands down. For in giving the gift, Denalyn gave hope.

A Love Worth Giving

LOVE PATIENTLY ACCEPTS ALL THINGS.
IT ALWAYS TRUSTS, ALWAYS HOPES, AND
ALWAYS ENDURES.

1 Corinthians 13:7 NCV

"Just Wonderful!"

Tucked away in the cedar chest of my memory is the image of a robust and rather rotund children's Bible class teacher in a small West Texas church. She wore black eyeglasses that peaked on the corners like a masquerade mask. Silver streaked through her black hair like a vein on the wall of a mine. She smelled like my mom's makeup and smiled like a kid on Christmas when she saw us coming to her class. Low-heeled shoes contained her thick ankles, but nothing contained her great passion. Hugs as we entered and hugs as we left. She knew all of us by name and made class so fun we'd rather miss the ice cream truck than Sunday school.

Here is why I tell you about her. She enjoyed giving us each a can of crayons and a sketch of Jesus torn from a coloring book. We each had our own can, mind you, reassigned from cupboard duty to classroom. What had held peaches or spinach now held a dozen or so Crayolas.

"Take the crayons I gave you," she would instruct, "and color Jesus." And so we would.

We didn't illustrate pictures of ourselves; we colored the Son of God. We didn't pirate crayons from other cans; we used what she gave us. This was the fun of it. "Do the best you can with the can you get." No blue for the sky? Make it purple. If Jesus's hair is blond instead of brown, the teacher won't mind. She loaded the can.

She taught us to paint Jesus with our own colors. . . .

Judging by her praise, you'd think her class roll had names like Rembrandt and van Gogh. One by one she waved the just-colored Christs in the air. "Wonderful work, Max. Just wonderful!"

Cure for the Common Life

THE HUMBLE HEART *honors* OTHERS.

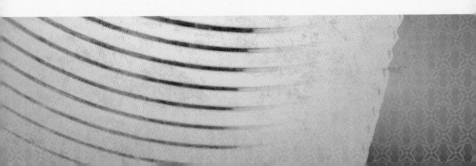

A Mission of
Mercy and Hope

Does God use common people?

Edith would say yes.

Edith Hayes was a spry eighty-year-old with thinning white hair, a wiry five-foot frame, and an unquenchable compassion for South Florida's cancer patients. I was fresh out of seminary in 1979 and sitting in an office of unpacked books when she walked in and introduced herself: "My name is Edith, and I help cancer patients." She extended her hand. I offered a chair. She politely declined. "Too busy. You'll see my team here at the church building every Tuesday morning. You're welcome to come, but if you come, we'll put you to work."

Her team, I came to learn, included a hundred or so silver-haired women who occupied themselves with the unglamorous concern of sore seepage. They made cancer wounds their mission, stitching together truckloads of disposable pads each Tuesday, then delivering them to patients throughout the week.

Edith rented an alley apartment, lived on her late husband's pension, wore glasses that magnified her pupils, and ducked applause like artillery fire. She would have fit in well with common folk like Peter and the disciples.

Outlive Your Life

YOU ARE SPECIAL

Let me tell you about a Chinese orphanage for the deaf and mute. China's one-child policy has a way of weeding out the weak. Males are selected over females. Healthy babies outrank the impaired. Chinese children who cannot speak or hear stand little chance of a healthy, productive life. Every message tells them, "You don't matter."

So when someone says otherwise, they melt. Chinese missionary John Bentley describes such a moment. Deaf orphans in Hunan province were given a Mandarin translation of a children's book I wrote entitled *You Are Special*. The story describes Punchinello, a wooden person in a village of wooden people. The villagers had a practice of sticking stars on the achievers and dots on the strugglers. Punchinello had so many dots that people gave him more dots for no reason at all.

But then he met Eli, his maker. Eli affirmed him, telling him to disregard the opinion of others. "I made you," he explained. "I don't make mistakes."

Punchinello had never heard such words. When he did, his dots began to fall off. And when the children in the

=====
AT A CERTAIN POINT
EVERYONE STARTED CRYING. I COULD NOT
UNDERSTAND THIS REACTION.
=====

Chinese orphanage heard such words, their worlds began to change. I'll let John describe the moment.

> When they first distributed these books to the children and staff of the deaf school, the most bizarre thing happened. At a certain point everyone started crying. I could not understand this reaction. . . . Americans are somewhat used to the idea of positive reinforcement. . . . Not so

in China and particularly not for these children who are virtually abandoned and considered valueless by their natural parents because they were born "broken." When the idea came through in the reading that they are special simply because they were made by a loving Creator . . . everyone started crying—including their teachers! It was wild. [3]

Fearless

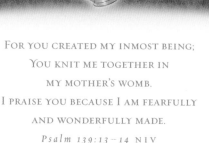

FOR YOU CREATED MY INMOST BEING;
YOU KNIT ME TOGETHER IN
MY MOTHER'S WOMB.
I PRAISE YOU BECAUSE I AM FEARFULLY
AND WONDERFULLY MADE.
Psalm 139:13–14 NIV

SOME PEOPLE LOVE YOU BECAUSE OF *you*.
God LOVES YOU BECAUSE HE IS HE.

6

CHANGED
BY COURAGE

ARE YOU DOING FOR GOD
WHAT HE COULD NOT DO ALONE?

BEAUTY IN A DEATH CAMP

CHARACTER AND COURAGE

A TRUE HERO

AMAZING HUMAN BEINGS

THANKS FOR THE COURAGE

BEAUTY IN A DEATH CAMP

It's difficult to find beauty in death. It's even more difficult to find beauty in a death camp. Especially Auschwitz. Four million Jews died there in World War II. A halfton of human hair is still preserved. The showers that sprayed poison gas still stand.

But for all the ugly memories of Auschwitz there is one of beauty. It's the memory Franciszek Gajowniczek has of Maximilian Kolbe.

In February 1941 Kolbe was incarcerated at Auschwitz. He was a Franciscan priest. In the harshness of the slaughterhouse he maintained the gentleness of Christ. He shared his food. He gave up his bunk. He prayed for his captors. One could call him the "Saint of Auschwitz."

In July of that same year there was an escape from the prison. It was the custom at Auschwitz to kill ten prisoners for every one who escaped. All the prisoners would be gathered in the courtyard, and the commandant would randomly select ten men from the ranks. These victims would be immediately taken to a cell where they would receive no food or water until they died.

The commandant begins his selection. At each selection another prisoner steps forward to fill the sinister quota. The tenth name he calls is Gajowniczek.

As the SS officers check the numbers of the condemned, one of the condemned begins to sob. "My wife and my children," he weeps.

The officers turn as they hear movement among the prisoners. The guards raise their rifles. The dogs tense, anticipating a command to attack. A prisoner has left his row and is pushing his way to the front.

It is Kolbe. No fear on his face. No hesitancy in his step. The capo shouts at him to stop or be shot. "I want to talk to the commander," he says calmly. For some reason the

---

IN THE HARSHNESS OF THE SLAUGHTERHOUSE
HE MAINTAINED THE GENTLENESS OF CHRIST.

---

officer doesn't club or kill him. Kolbe stops a few paces from the commandant, removes his hat, and looks the German officer in the eye.

"Herr Commandant, I wish to make a request, please."

That no one shot him is a miracle.

"I want to die in the place of this prisoner." He points at the sobbing Gajowniczek. The audacious request is presented without stammer.

"I have no wife and children. Besides, I am old and not good for anything. He's in better condition." Kolbe knew well the Nazi mentality.

"Who are you?" the officer asks.

"A Catholic priest."

The block is stunned. The commandant, uncharacteristically speechless. After a moment, he barks, "Request granted."

Prisoners were never allowed to speak. Gajowniczek says, "I could only thank him with my eyes. I was stunned and could hardly grasp what was going on. The immensity of it: I, the condemned, am to live and someone else willingly and voluntarily offers his life for me—a stranger. Is this some dream?"

The Saint of Auschwitz outlived the other nine. In fact, he didn't die of thirst or starvation. He died only after carbolic acid was injected into his veins. It was August 14, 1941.

Gajowniczek survived the Holocaust. He made his way back to his hometown. Every year, however, he goes back to Auschwitz. Every August 14 he goes back to say thank you to the man who died in his place.

In his backyard there is a plaque. A plaque he carved with his own hands. A tribute to Maximilian Kolbe—the man who died so he could live. [1]

Six Hours One Friday

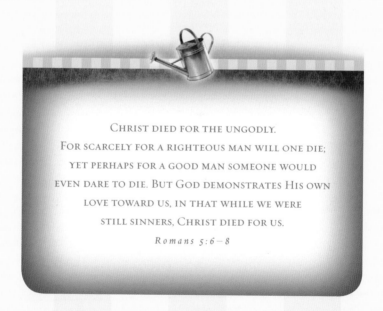

CHRIST DIED FOR THE UNGODLY.
FOR SCARCELY FOR A RIGHTEOUS MAN WILL ONE DIE;
YET PERHAPS FOR A GOOD MAN SOMEONE WOULD
EVEN DARE TO DIE. BUT GOD DEMONSTRATES HIS OWN
LOVE TOWARD US, IN THAT WHILE WE WERE
STILL SINNERS, CHRIST DIED FOR US.

Romans 5:6−8

Blessed ARE THOSE WHO HOLD THEIR EARTHLY POSSESSIONS IN *open* PALMS.

CHARACTER
AND COURAGE

Mention courage and I think of a little-known but gutsy young man named Paul Keating. On a cold night in February 1980, twenty-seven-year-old Keating was walking home in Manhattan's Greenwich Village when he saw two armed muggers robbing a college student. Keating, a gentle, much-admired photographer for *Time* magazine, had every reason to avoid trouble. He didn't know the student. No one knew he saw the crime. He was outnumbered. He had nothing to gain and much to lose by taking the risk, and yet he jumped on the muggers. The victim escaped and ran to a nearby deli to call for help. Moments later, two shots cracked the night, and the muggers fled. Paul Keating was found dead on the pavement.

The city of New York posthumously awarded him a medal of heroism. I think you'll agree with the commentary offered by Mayor Edward Koch at the ceremony: "Nobody was watching Paul Keating on the street that night. Nobody made him step forward in the time of crisis. He did it because of who he was." [2]

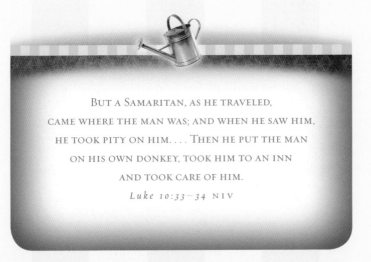

BUT A SAMARITAN, AS HE TRAVELED,
CAME WHERE THE MAN WAS; AND WHEN HE SAW HIM,
HE TOOK PITY ON HIM. . . . THEN HE PUT THE MAN
ON HIS OWN DONKEY, TOOK HIM TO AN INN
AND TOOK CARE OF HIM.

Luke 10:33–34 NIV

A TRUE HERO

Artful Eddie lacked nothing.

He was the slickest of the slick lawyers. He was one of the roars of the Roaring Twenties. A crony of Al Capone, he ran the gangster's dog tracks. He mastered the simple technique of fixing the race by overfeeding seven dogs and betting on the eighth.

Wealth. Status. Style. Artful Eddie lacked nothing.

Then why did he turn himself in? Why did he offer to squeal on Capone? What was his motive? Didn't Eddie know the sure-fire consequences of ratting on the mob?

He knew, but he'd made up his mind.

What did he have to gain? What could society give him that he didn't have? He had money, power, prestige.

What was the hitch?

Eddie revealed the hitch. His son. Eddie had spent his life with the despicable. He had smelled the stench of the underground long enough. For his son, he wanted more. He wanted to give his son a name. And to give his son a

---

EDDIE WAS WILLING TO TAKE A RISK SO THAT HIS SON COULD HAVE A CLEAN SLATE.

---

name, he would have to clear his own. Eddie was willing to take a risk so that his son could have a clean slate. Artful Eddie never saw his dream come true. After Eddie squealed, the mob remembered. Two shotgun blasts silenced him forever.

Was it worth it?

For the son it was. Artful Eddie's boy lived up to the sacrifice. His is one of the best-known names in the world.

Had Eddie lived to see his son, Butch, grow up, he would have been proud. He would have been proud of Butch's appointment to Annapolis. He would have been proud of the commissioning as a World War II Navy pilot. He would have been proud as he read of his son downing five bombers in the Pacific night and saving the lives of hundreds of crewmen on the carrier Lexington. The name was cleared. The Congressional Medal of Honor that Butch received was proof.

When people say the name O'Hare in Chicago, they don't think gangsters—they think aviation heroism.

And the Angels Were Silent

FOR ALL HAVE SINNED AND FALL SHORT
OF THE GLORY OF GOD, AND ARE JUSTIFIED FREELY BY
HIS GRACE THROUGH REDEMPTION THAT
CAME BY CHRIST JESUS.

Romans 3:23−24 NIV

WHAT IS *grace*? IT'S WHAT SOMEONE GIVES US
OUT OF THE *goodness* OF HIS HEART,
NOT OUT OF THE *perfection* OF OURS.

AMAZING
HUMAN BEINGS

Dan Mazur considered himself lucky. Most other people would have considered him crazy. He stood within a two-hour hike of the summit of Mount Everest, a thousand feet from realizing a lifelong dream. Every year the fittest adventurers on earth set their sights on the twenty-nine-thousand-foot peak. Every year some die in the effort. The top of Everest isn't known for its hospitality. Climbers call the realm above twenty-six thousand feet "the death zone." Temperatures hover below zero. Sudden blizzards stir blinding snow. The atmosphere is oxygen starved. Corpses dot the mountaintop. A British climber had died ten days prior to Mazur's attempt. Forty climbers who could have helped chose not to do so. They passed him on the way to the summit. Everest can be cruel. Still, Mazur felt lucky. He and two colleagues were within eyesight of the top. Years of planning. Six weeks of climbing, and now at 7:30 a.m., May 25, 2006, the air was still, morning sun brilliant, energy and hopes high.

That's when a flash of color caught Mazur's eye: a bit of yellow fabric on the ridgetop. He first thought it was a tent. He soon saw it was a person, a man precariously perched on an eight-thousand-foot razor-edge rock. His gloves were off, jacket unzipped, hands exposed, chest bare. Oxygen deprivation can swell the brain and stir hallucinations. Mazur knew this man had no idea where he was, so he walked toward him and called out.

"Can you tell me your name?"

"Yes," the man answered, sounding pleased. "I can. My name is Lincoln Hall."

Mazur was shocked. He recognized this name. Twelve hours earlier he'd heard the news on the radio: "Lincoln Hall is dead on the mountain. His team has left his body on the slope."

And yet, after spending the night in twenty-below chill and oxygen-stingy air, Lincoln Hall was still alive. Mazur was face to face with a miracle.

He was also face to face with a choice. A rescue attempt had profound risks. The descent was already treacherous, even more so with the dead weight of a dying man.

THE THREE CLIMBERS MIGHT SACRIFICE THEIR EVEREST FOR NAUGHT.

Besides, how long would Hall survive? No one knew. The three climbers might sacrifice their Everest for naught. They had to choose: abandon their dream or abandon Lincoln Hall.

They chose to abandon their dream. The three turned their backs on the peak and inched their way down the mountain.

Lincoln Hall survived the trip down Mount Everest. Thanks to Dan Mazur, he lived to be reunited with his wife and sons in New Zealand. A television reporter asked Lincoln's wife what she thought of the rescuers, the men who surrendered their summit to save her husband's life. She tried to answer, but the words stuck in her throat. After several moments and with tear-filled eyes, she offered, "Well, there's one amazing human being. And the other men with him. The world needs more people like that." [3]

Every Day Deserves a Chance

THOSE WHO *suffer* BELONG TO ALL OF US.

AND IF ALL OF US RESPOND, THERE IS *hope*.

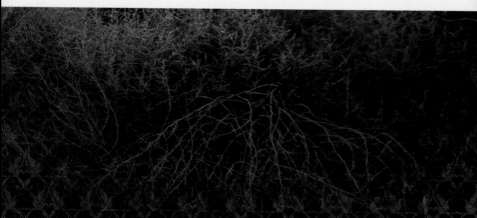

THANKS FOR THE COURAGE

I'm writing to say thanks. I wish I could thank you personally, but I don't know where you are. I wish I could call you, but I don't know your name. If I knew your appearance, I'd look for you, but your face is fuzzy in my memory. But I'll never forget what you did.

There you were, leaning against your pickup in the West Texas oil field. An engineer of some sort. A supervisor on the job. Your khakis and clean shirt set you apart from us roustabouts. In the oil field pecking order, we were at the bottom. You were the boss. We were the workers. You read the blueprints. We dug the ditches. You inspected the pipe. We laid it. You ate with the bosses in the shed. We ate with each other in the shade.

Except that day.

I remember wondering why you did it.

We weren't much to look at. What wasn't sweaty was oily. Faces burnt from the sun; skin black from the grease. Didn't bother me, though. I was there only for the summer. A high-school boy earning good money laying

---

LIKE THE OTHERS, I GROANED
WHEN I SAW YOU COMING.

---

pipe. For me, it was a summer job. For the others, it was a way of life. Most were illegal immigrants from Mexico. Others were drifters, bouncing across the prairie as rootless as tumbleweeds.

We weren't much to listen to, either. Our language was sandpaper coarse. After lunch, we'd light the cigarettes and begin the jokes. Someone always had a deck of cards with lacy-clad girls on the back. For thirty minutes in the heat of the day, the oil patch became Las Vegas—replete with foul language, dirty stories, blackjack, and barstools that doubled as lunch pails.

In the middle of such a game, you approached us. I thought you had a job for us that couldn't wait another few minutes. Like the others, I groaned when I saw you coming.

You were nervous. You shifted your weight from one leg to the other as you began to speak.

"Uh, fellows," you started.

We turned and looked up at you.

"I, uh, I just wanted, uh, to invite . . ."

You were way out of your comfort zone. I had no idea what you might be about to say, but I knew that it had nothing to do with work.

"I just wanted to tell you that, uh, our church is having a service tonight and, uh . . ."

What? I couldn't believe it. *He's talking church? Out here? With us?*

"I wanted to invite any of you to come along."

Silence. Screaming silence. The same silence you'd hear if a nun asked a madam if she could use the brothel for a mass. The same silence you'd hear if an IRS representative invited the Mafia to a seminar on tax integrity.

Several guys stared at the dirt. A few shot glances at the others. Snickers rose just inches from the surface.

"Well, that's it. Uh, if any of you want to go . . . uh, let me know."

After you turned and left, we turned and laughed. We called you "reverend," "preacher," and "the pope." We poked fun at each other, daring one another to go. You became the butt of the day's jokes.

I'm sure you knew that. I'm sure you went back to your truck knowing the only good you'd done was to make a good fool out of yourself. If that's what you thought, then you were wrong.

That's the reason for this letter.

I want you to know that at least one of the seeds fell into a fertile crevice.

Some five years later, a college sophomore was struggling with a decision. He had drifted from the faith given to him by his parents. He wanted to come back. He wanted to come home. But the price was high. His friends might laugh. His habits would have to change. His reputation would have to be overcome.

Could he do it? Did he have the courage?

That's when I thought of you. As I sat in my dorm room late one night, looking for the guts to do what I knew was right, I thought of you.

I thought of how your love for God had been greater than your love for your reputation.

I thought of how your obedience had been greater than your common sense.

I remembered how you had cared more about making disciples than about making a good first impression. And when I thought of you, your memory became my motivation.

So I came home.

I've told your story dozens of times to thousands of people. Each time the reaction is the same: The audience becomes a sea of smiles, and heads bob in understanding. Some smile because they think of the "clean-shirted engineers" in their lives. They remember the neighbor who brought the cake, the aunt who wrote the letter, the teacher who listened. . . .

I'M SURE YOU WALKED AWAY THAT DAY THINKING THAT YOUR EFFORTS HAD BEEN WASTED.

Others smile because they have done what you did. And they, too, wonder if their "lunchtime loyalty" was worth the effort.

You wondered that. What you did that day wasn't much. And I'm sure you walked away that day thinking that your efforts had been wasted.

They weren't.

So I'm writing to say thanks. Thanks for the example. Thanks for the courage.

In the Eye of the Storm

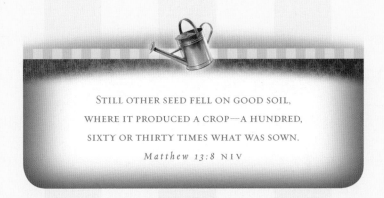

STILL OTHER SEED FELL ON GOOD SOIL,
WHERE IT PRODUCED A CROP—A HUNDRED,
SIXTY OR THIRTY TIMES WHAT WAS SOWN.
Matthew 13:8 NIV

7

CHANGED
BY WISDOM

GOD CAN USE AN ORDINARY LIFE
TO BRING EXTRAORDINARY BLESSING
INTO THE WORLD.

SHARING THE KNOWLEDGE
OF CHRIST

WE'VE BROKEN YOUR PLATE

A WISE RESPONSE

SIMPLE WISDOM

BLESSED BY WISE PARENTS

A WISE AND LOVING DAD

ALONG FOR THE RIDE

SHARING THE KNOWLEDGE OF CHRIST

Russia of the early 1950s needed little excuse to imprison her citizens.

Let a person question a decision of Stalin or speak against the Communist regime, and he could find himself walking the frozen tundra behind the barbed wires of a Soviet concentration camp. Boris Kornfeld did. No known record of his crime survives, only the sketchy details of his life. Born a Jew. Trained as a physician and befriended by a believer in Christ.

With ample time on their hands, the two men engaged in long, rigorous discussions. Kornfeld began to connect the promised Messiah of the old covenant with the Nazarene of the new. Following Jesus went against every fiber of his ancestry, but in the end he chose to do so.

The decision cost him his life.

He saw a guard stealing bread from a dying man. Prior to his conversion, Kornfeld never would have reported the crime. Now his conscience compelled him to do so. It was only a matter of time before the other guards would get

---

FOR THE FIRST TIME IN HIS LIFE, HE HAD NO FEAR OF DEATH OR ETERNITY.

---

even. Kornfeld, even in danger, was at complete peace. For the first time in his life, he had no fear of death or eternity. His only desire was to tell someone about his discovery before he lost his life.

An opportunity came in the form of a cancer patient, a fellow prisoner who was recovering from abdominal surgery. Left alone with him in the recovery room, Kornfeld urgently whispered his story. He poured out every detail. The young man was stirred yet so groggy from the anesthesia that he fell asleep. When he awoke, he asked to see the physician. It was too late. During the night someone had dealt the doctor eight blows on the head with a plasterer's hammer. Colleagues had tried to save his life but couldn't.

There, in the quiet camp hospital recovery room, the doctor sat by his patient's bedside, dispensing compassion and peace. Dr. Kornfeld passionately related the story of his conversion to Christianity, his words flavored with conviction. The patient was hot and feverish, yet alert enough to ponder Dr. Kornfeld's words. He would later write that he sensed a "mystical knowledge" in the doctor's voice.

The "mystical knowledge" transformed the young patient. He embraced Kornfeld's Christ and later celebrated in verse with this joyous affirmation: God of Universe! I believe again! [1]

The patient survived the camps and began to write about his prison experience, disclosing the gulag horror. One exposé after another: *One Day in the Life of Ivan Denisovich, The Gulag Archipelago, Live Not by Lies.* Some attribute the collapse of Eastern Communism, in part, to his writings. But were it not for the suffering of Kornfeld, we'd have never known the brilliance of his young convert: Alexander Solzhenitsyn.

What man meant for evil, God, yet again, used for good.

Fearless

FOR GOD HAS NOT GIVEN US A SPIRIT OF FEAR,
BUT OF POWER AND OF LOVE AND
OF A SOUND MIND.

2 Timothy 1:7

WE'VE BROKEN
YOUR PLATE

It was past midnight in Dalton, Georgia, as I stood in a dimly lit phone booth making a call to my folks. My first summer job away from home wasn't panning out as it was supposed to. The work was hard. My two best friends had quit and gone back to Texas, and I was bunking in the Salvation Army until I could find an apartment.

For a big, tough nineteen-year-old, I sure felt small.

The voices of my mom and dad had never sounded so sweet. And although I tried to hide it, my loneliness was obvious. I had promised my parents that if they'd let me go, I'd stick it out for the whole summer. But now those three months looked like eternity.

As I explained my plight, I could tell my mom wanted

me to come home. But just as she said, "Why don't you come . . . ," my dad, who was on the extension, interrupted her. "We'd love for you to come back, but we've already broken your plate."

(That was West Texas talk for "We love you, Max, but it's time to grow up.")

It takes a wise father to know when to push his son out of the nest. It's painful, but it has to be done. I'll always be thankful that my dad gave me wings and then made me use them.

On the Anvil

WANT TO ENJOY GOD'S *generosity*?

THEN LET *others* ENJOY YOURS.

A Wise Response

Come with me to Paris, France, 1954. Elie Wiesel is a correspondent for a Jewish newspaper. A decade earlier he was a prisoner in a Jewish concentration camp. A decade later he would be known as the author of *Night*, the Pulitzer Prize-winning account of the Holocaust. Eventually he'll be awarded the Congressional Medal of Achievement and the Nobel Peace Prize.

But tonight Elie Wiesel is a twenty-six-year-old unknown newspaper correspondent. He is about to interview the French author François Mauriac, who is a devout Christian. Mauriac is France's most recent Nobel laureate for literature and an expert on French political life.

Wiesel shows up at Mauriac's apartment, nervous and chain-smoking—his emotions still frayed from the German horror, his comfort as a writer still raw. The older Mauriac tries to put him at ease. He invites Wiesel in, and the two sit in the small room. Before Wiesel can ask a question, however, Mauriac, a staunch Roman Catholic, begins to speak about his favorite subject: Jesus. Wiesel grows uneasy. The name of Jesus is a pressed thumb on his infected wounds.

Wiesel tries to reroute the conversation but can't. It is as though everything in creation leads back to Jesus. Jerusalem? Jerusalem is where Jesus ministered. The Old Testament? Because of Jesus, the Old is now enriched by the New. Mauriac turns every topic toward the Messiah. The anger in Wiesel begins to heat. The Christian anti-Semitism he'd grown up with, the layers of grief from Sighet, Auschwitz, and Buchenwald—it all boils over. He puts away his pen, shuts his notebook, and stands up angrily.

> "Sir," he said to the still-seated Mauriac, "you speak of Christ. Christians love to speak of him. The passion of Christ, the agony of Christ, the death of Christ. In your religion, that is all you speak of. Well, I want you to know that ten years ago, not very far from here, I knew Jewish children every one of whom suffered a

thousand times more, six million times more, than Christ on the cross. And we don't speak about them. Can you understand that, sir? We don't speak about them." [2]

Mauriac is stunned. Wiesel turns and marches out the door. Mauriac sits in shock, his woolen blanket still around him. The young reporter is pressing the eleva-

THE NAME OF JESUS IS A PRESSED THUMB ON HIS INFECTED WOUNDS.

tor button when Mauriac appears in the hall. He gently reaches for Wiesel's arm. "Come back," he implores. Wiesel agrees, and the two sit on the sofa. At this point Mauriac begins to weep. He looks at Wiesel but says nothing. Just tears.

Wiesel starts to apologize. Mauriac will have nothing of it. Instead he urges his young friend to talk. He wants to hear about it—the camps, the trains, the deaths. He asks Wiesel why he hasn't put this to paper. Wiesel tells him the pain is too severe. He's made a vow of silence. The older man tells him to break it and speak out.

The evening changed them both. The drama became the soil of a lifelong friendship.

They corresponded until Mauriac's death in 1970. "I owe François Mauriac my career," Wiesel has said . . . and it was to Mauriac that Wiesel sent the first manuscript of *Night*.

What if Mauriac had kept the door shut? Would anyone have blamed him? Cut by the sharp words of Wiesel, he could have become impatient with the angry young man and have been glad to be rid of him. But he didn't and he wasn't. He reacted decisively, quickly, and lovingly.

A Love Worth Giving

WITH GOD, EVERY *day* MATTERS,
EVERY *person* COUNTS.

SIMPLE WISDOM

Oliver Cromwell's secretary was dispatched to the continent on some important business. He stayed one night at a seaport town, and tossed on his bed, unable to sleep.

According to an old custom, a servant slept in his room, and on this occasion slept soundly enough. After some time the secretary awakened his servant and complained of insomnia.

"I am so afraid something will go wrong with our work."

"Master," said the valet, "may I ask a question or two?"

"To be sure."

"Did God rule the world before we were born?"

"Most assuredly He did."

"And will He rule it after we are dead?"

"Certainly He will."

"Then, master, why not let Him rule the present too?"

The secretary's faith was stirred, peace was the result, and in a few minutes both he and his servant were in sound sleep. [3]

From the sermon "Making Sense Out of Chaos".

Blessed by Wise Parents

Uncommon are the parents who attempt to learn the God-given talents of their children—and blessed are their children.

Read my name among the blessed. Crankcase oil coursed my dad's veins. He repaired oil-field engines for a living and rebuilt car engines for fun. He worked in grease and bolts like sculptors work in clay; they were his media of choice. Dad loved machines.

But God gave him a mechanical moron, a son who couldn't differentiate between a differential and a brake disc. My dad tried to teach me. I tried to learn. Honestly, I did. But more than once I actually dozed off under the car on which we were working.

Machines anesthetized me. But books fascinated me. I biked to the library a thousand times. What does a mechanic do with a son who loves books?

He gives him a library card. Buys him a few volumes for Christmas. Places a lamp by his bed so he can read at night. Pays tuition so his son can study college literature in high school. My dad did that. You know what he didn't do? Never once did he say, "Why can't you be a mechanic like your dad and granddad?" Maybe he understood my bent. Or maybe he didn't want me to die of hunger.

Cure for the Common Life

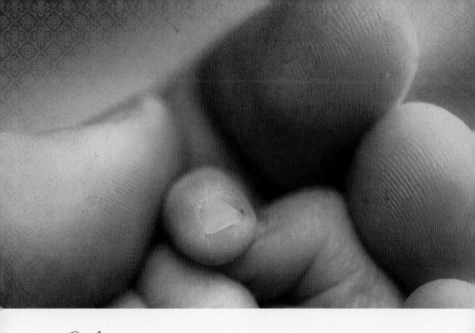

God PLACED HIS HAND ON THE SHOULDER OF HUMANITY
AND SAID, "YOU'RE SOMETHING *special*."

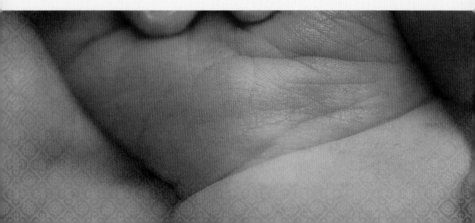

A Wise and Loving Dad

In his delightful book *The Dance of Hope*, my friend Bill Frey tells of a blind student named John, whom he tutored at the University of Colorado in 1951. One day Bill asked John how he had become blind. The sightless student described an accident that had happened in his teenage years. The tragedy took not just the boy's sight but also his hope. He told Bill, "I was bitter and angry with God for letting it happen, and I took my anger out on everyone around me. I felt that since I had no future, I wouldn't lift a finger on my own behalf. Let others wait on me. I shut my bedroom door and refused to come out except for meals."

His admission surprised Bill. The student he assisted displayed no bitterness or anger. He asked John to explain the change. John credited his father. Weary of the pity party and ready for his son to get on with life, he reminded the boy of the impending winter and told him to mount the storm windows. "Do the work before I get home or else," the dad insisted, slamming the door on the way out.

John reacted with anger. Muttering and cursing and groping all the way to the garage, he found the windows, stepladder, and tools and went to work. "They'll be sorry when I fall off my ladder and break my neck." But he didn't fall. Little by little he inched around the house and finished the chore.

The assignment achieved the dad's goal. John reluctantly realized he could still work and began to reconstruct his life. Years later he learned something else about that day. When he shared this detail with Bill, his blind eyes misted. "I later discovered that at no time during the day had my father ever been more than four or five feet from my side." [4]

ALONG FOR
THE RIDE

While in Colorado for a week's vacation, our family teamed up with several others and decided to ascend the summit of a fourteen-thousand-foot peak. We would climb it the easy way. Drive above the timberline and tackle the final mile by foot. You hearty hikers would have been bored, but for a family with three small girls, it was about all we could take.

The journey was as tiring as it was beautiful. I was reminded how the air was thin and my waist was not.

Our four-year-old Sara had it doubly difficult. A tumble in the first few minutes left her with a skinned knee and a timid step. She didn't want to walk. Actually, she refused to walk. She wanted to ride. First on my back, then in

Mom's arms, then my back, then a friend's back, then my back, then Mom's . . . well, you get the picture.

As I tried, unsuccessfully, to convince Sara to walk, I tried describing what we were going to see. "It will be

> I DIDN'T SAY ANYTHING BECAUSE
> I'M GETTING THE SAME TREATMENT.

so pretty," I told her. "You'll see all the mountains and the sky and the trees." No luck—she wanted to be carried. Still a good idea, however. Even if it didn't work. Nothing puts power in the journey like a vision of the mountaintop.

Our group finally made it up the mountain. We spent an hour or so at the top, taking pictures and enjoying the view. Later, on the way down, I heard little Sara exclaim proudly, "I did it!"

I chuckled. *No you didn't,* I thought. *Your mom and I did it. Friends and family got you up this mountain. You didn't do it.*

But I didn't say anything. I didn't say anything because I'm getting the same treatment. So are you. We may think we are climbing, but we are riding. Riding on the back of the Father who saw us fall. Riding on the back of the Father who wants us to make it home. A Father who doesn't get angry when we get weary.

When God Whispers Your Name

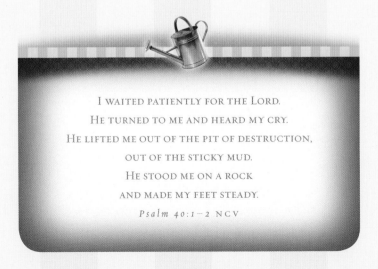

I WAITED PATIENTLY FOR THE LORD.
HE TURNED TO ME AND HEARD MY CRY.
HE LIFTED ME OUT OF THE PIT OF DESTRUCTION,
OUT OF THE STICKY MUD.
HE STOOD ME ON A ROCK
AND MADE MY FEET STEADY.

Psalm 40:1–2 NCV

8

CHANGED
BY FRIENDSHIP

GOD OUTFITS HIS FOLLOWERS
TO TOUCH HEARTS.

SHE BOWED TO HER FRIEND

FRIENDS IN THE FAITH

A FRIEND INDEED

BEST FRIENDS

WE HAVE A FRIEND IN GOD

FEASTING ON FRIENDSHIP

"IT'S GOING TO BE OKAY"

SHE BOWED TO
HER FRIEND

For thirteen years Esther Kim had one dream. The Summer Olympics. She wanted to represent the United States on the Olympic taekwondo squad.

From the age of eight, she spent every available hour in training. In fact, it was in training that she met and made her best friend, Kay Poe. The two worked so hard for so long that no one was surprised when they both qualified for the 2000 Olympic trials in Colorado Springs.

Everyone, however, was surprised when they were placed in the same division. They'd never competed against each other, but when the number of divisions was reduced, they found their names on the same bracket. It would be just a matter of events before they found themselves on the same mat. One would win and one would lose. Only one could go to Australia.

As if the moment needed more drama, two facts put Esther Kim in a heartrending position. First, her friend Kay injured her leg in the match prior to theirs. Kay could scarcely walk, much less compete. Because of the injury Esther could defeat her friend with hardly any effort.

But then there was a second truth. Esther knew that Kay was the better fighter. If she took advantage of her crippled friend, the better athlete would stay home.

So what did she do? Esther stepped onto the floor and bowed to her friend and opponent. Both knew the meaning of the gesture. Esther forfeited her place. She considered the cause more important than the credit. [1]

A Love Worth Giving

FRIENDS IN THE FAITH

I am deeply appreciative of my heritage. It was through a small, West Texas Church of Christ that I came to know the Nazarene, the cross, and the Word. The congregation wasn't large, maybe two hundred on a good Sunday. Most of the families were like mine, blue-collar oil-field workers. But it was a loving church. When our family was sick, the members visited us. When we were absent, they called. And when this prodigal returned, they embraced me.

I deeply appreciate my heritage. But through the years, my faith has been supplemented by people of other groups. I wasn't long on God's ship before I found encouragement in other staterooms.

A Brazilian Pentecostal taught me about prayer. A British Anglican by the name of C. S. Lewis put muscle in my faith. A Southern Baptist helped me understand grace. One Presbyterian, Steve Brown, taught me about God's sovereignty while another, Frederick Buechner, taught me about God's passion. A Catholic, Brennan Manning, convinced me that Jesus is relentlessly tender. I'm a better husband because I read James Dobson and a better preacher because I listened to Chuck Swindoll.

In the Grip of Grace

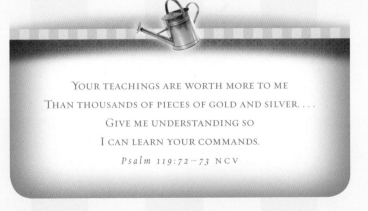

YOUR TEACHINGS ARE WORTH MORE TO ME
THAN THOUSANDS OF PIECES OF GOLD AND SILVER. . . .
GIVE ME UNDERSTANDING SO
I CAN LEARN YOUR COMMANDS.
Psalm 119:72–73 NCV

YOU OFFER A *gift* TO SOCIETY

THAT NO ONE ELSE BRINGS.

IF YOU DON'T BRING IT, IT WON'T BE BROUGHT.

A FRIEND INDEED

Little Blake Rogers can help us understand Jesus's great act of grace. He offered a remotely similar gift to his friend Maura. Blake and Maura share a kindergarten class. One day she started humming. Her teacher appreciated the music but told Maura to stop. It's not polite to hum in class.

She couldn't. The song in her head demanded to be hummed. After several warnings, the teacher took decisive action. She moved Maura's clothespin from the green spot on the chart to the dreaded blue spot. This meant trouble.

And this meant a troubled Maura. Everyone else's clothespin hung in the green. Maura was blue, all by herself.

Blake tried to help. He patted her on the back, made funny faces, and offered comforting words. But nothing worked. Maura still felt alone. So Blake made the ultimate sacrifice. Making sure his teacher was watching, he began to hum. The teacher warned him to stop. He didn't. She had no choice but to move his clothespin out of the green and into the blue.

Blake smiled, and Maura stopped crying. She had a friend.

Cure for the Common Life

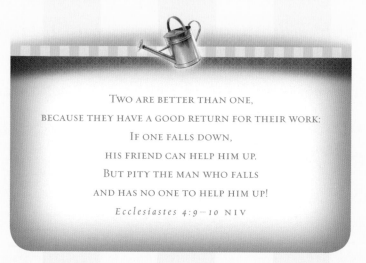

TWO ARE BETTER THAN ONE,
BECAUSE THEY HAVE A GOOD RETURN FOR THEIR WORK:
IF ONE FALLS DOWN,
HIS FRIEND CAN HELP HIM UP.
BUT PITY THE MAN WHO FALLS
AND HAS NO ONE TO HELP HIM UP!
Ecclesiastes 4:9–10 NIV

BEST FRIENDS

Standing before ten thousand eyes is Abraham Lincoln. An uncomfortable Abraham Lincoln. His discomfort comes not from the thought of delivering his first inaugural address but from the ambitious efforts of well-meaning tailors. He's unaccustomed to such attire—formal black dress coat, silk vest, black trousers, and a glossy top hat. He holds a huge ebony cane with a golden head the size of an egg.

He approaches the platform with hat in one hand and cane in the other. He doesn't know what to do with either one. In the nervous silence that comes after the applause and before the speech, he searches for a spot to place them. He finally leans the cane in a corner of the railing, but he still doesn't know what to do with the hat. He could lay it on the podium, but it would take up too much room. Perhaps the floor . . . no, too dirty.

Just then, and not a moment too soon, a man steps forward and takes the hat, returns to his seat, and listens intently to Lincoln's speech.

Who is he? Lincoln's dearest friend. The president said of him, "He and I are about the best friends in the world."

He was one of the strongest supporters of the early stages of Lincoln's presidency. He was given the honor of escorting Mrs. Lincoln in the inaugural grand ball. As the storm of the Civil War began to boil, many of Lincoln's friends left, but not this one. He amplified his loyalty by touring the South as Lincoln's peace ambassador. He begged Southerners not to secede and Northerners to rally behind the president.

His efforts were great, but the wave of anger was greater. The country did divide, and civil war bloodied the nation. Lincoln's friend never lived to see it. He died three months after Lincoln's inauguration. Wearied by his travels, he succumbed to a fever, and Lincoln was left to face the war alone.

Upon hearing the news of his friend's death, Lincoln wept openly and ordered the White House flag to be flown at half-staff. Some feel Lincoln's friend would have been chosen as his running mate in 1864 and would thus have become president following the assassination of the Great Emancipator.

No one will ever know about that. But we do know that Lincoln had one true friend. And we can only imagine the number of times the memory of him brought warmth to a cold Oval Office. He was a model of friendship.

He was also a model of forgiveness.

This friend could just as easily have been an enemy. Long before he and Lincoln were allies, they were competitors—politicians pursuing the same office. And unfortunately, their debates are better known than their friendship. The debates between Abraham Lincoln and his dear friend, Stephen A. Douglas.

He Still Moves Stones

WHAT IF WE INFILTRATED ALL CORNERS OF THE WORLD

WITH *God's love* AND LIFE?

WE HAVE A FRIEND
IN GOD

May I share a time when God gave me a message using the grammar of need? The birth of our first child coincided with the cancellation of our health insurance. I still don't understand how it happened. It had to do with the company being based in the U.S. and Jenna being born in Brazil. Denalyn and I were left with the joy of an eight-pound baby girl and the burden of a twenty-five-hundred-dollar hospital bill.

We settled the bill by draining a savings account. Thankful to be able to pay the debt but bewildered by the insurance problem, I wondered, "Is God trying to tell us something?"

A few weeks later the answer came. I spoke at a retreat for a small, happy church in Florida. A member of the congregation handed me an envelope and said, "This is for your family." Such gifts were not uncommon. We were accustomed to and grateful for these unsolicited donations, which usually amounted to fifty or a hundred dollars. I expected the amount to be comparable. But when I opened the envelope, the check was for (you guessed it) twenty-five hundred dollars.

Through the language of need, God spoke to me. It was as if he said, "Max, I'm involved in your life. I will take care of you."

He Chose the Nails

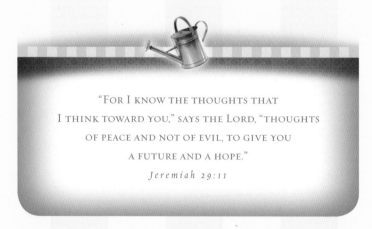

"For I know the thoughts that I think toward you," says the Lord, "thoughts of peace and not of evil, to give you a future and a hope."

Jeremiah 29:11

FEASTING ON FRIENDSHIP

My first ministry position was in Miami, Florida. In our congregation we had more than our share of southern ladies who loved to cook. I fit in well because I was a single guy who loved to eat. The church was fond of having Sunday evening potluck dinners, and about once a quarter they *feasted*.

Some church dinners live up to the "potluck" name. The cooks empty the pot, and you try your luck. Not so with this church. Our potlucks were major events. Area grocery stores asked us to advise them in advance so they could stock their shelves. Cookbook sales went up. People never before seen in the pews could be found in the food line. For the women it was an unofficial cook-off, and for the men it was an unabashed pig-out.

My, it was good, a veritable cornucopia of Corningware. Juicy ham bathed in pineapple, baked beans, pickled relish, pecan pie . . . (Oops, I just drooled on my computer keyboard.) Ever wondered why there are so many hefty preachers? You enter the ministry for meals like those.

As a bachelor I counted on potluck dinners for my survival strategy. While others were planning what to cook, I was studying the storage techniques of camels. Know-

---

THE WAY THOSE LADIES ACTED,
YOU WOULD'VE THOUGHT I BROUGHT
THE THANKSGIVING TURKEY.

---

ing I should bring something, I'd make it a point to raid my kitchen shelves on Sunday afternoon. The result was pitiful: One time I took a half-empty jar of Planters peanuts; another time I made a half-dozen jelly sandwiches. One of my better offerings was an unopened sack of chips; a more meager gift was a can of tomato soup, also unopened.

Wasn't much, but no one ever complained. In fact, the way those ladies acted, you would've thought I brought the Thanksgiving turkey. They'd take my jar of peanuts and set it on the long table with the rest of the food and hand me a plate. "Go ahead, Max, don't be bashful. Fill up your plate." And I would! Mashed potatoes and gravy. Roast beef. Fried chicken. I took a little bit of everything, except the peanuts.

I came like a pauper and ate like a king!

Cast of Characters

I SAY TO YOU THAT MANY WILL COME FROM THE EAST
AND THE WEST, AND WILL TAKE THEIR PLACES
AT THE FEAST WITH ABRAHAM, ISAAC, AND JACOB
IN THE KINGDOM OF HEAVEN.

Matthew 8:11

"It's Going to Be Okay"

Bill was sixteen years old when his dad suffered a health crisis and consequently had to leave his business. Even after Mr. Tucker regained his health, the Tucker family struggled financially, barely getting by.

Mr. Tucker, an entrepreneurial sort, came up with an idea. He won the bid to reupholster the chairs at the local movie theater. This stunned his family. He had never stitched a seat. He didn't even own a sewing apparatus. Still, he found someone to teach him the skill and located an industrial-strength machine. The family scraped together every cent they had to buy it. They drained savings accounts and dug coins out of the sofa. Finally they had enough.

It was a fine day when Bill rode with his dad to pick up the equipment. Bill remembers a jovial, hour-long trip discussing the bright horizons this new opportunity afforded them. They loaded the machine in the back of their truck and secured it right behind the cab. Mr. Tucker then invited his son to drive home. I'll let Bill tell you what happened:

> "As we were driving along, we were excited, and I, like any sixteen-year-old driver, was probably not paying enough attention to my speed. Just as we were turning on the cloverleaf to get on the expressway, I will never ever, ever forget watching that sewing machine, which was already top-heavy, begin to tip. I slammed on the brakes, but it was too late. I saw it go over the side. I jumped out and ran around the back of the truck. As I rounded the corner, I saw our hope and our dream lying on its side in pieces. And then I saw my dad just looking. All of his risk and all of his endeavor and all

of his struggling and all of his dream, all of his hope to take care of his family was lying there, shattered.

"You know what comes next, don't you? 'Stupid, punk kid driving too fast, not paying attention, ruined the family by taking away our livelihood.' But that's not what he said. He looked right at me. 'Oh, Bill, I am so sorry.' And he walked over, put his arms around me, and said, 'Son, this is going to be okay.'" [2]

3:16: The Numbers of Hope

WHERE GOD'S LOVE IS, THERE IS NO FEAR, BECAUSE GOD'S PERFECT LOVE DRIVES OUT FEAR.

1 John 4:18 NCV

ENDNOTES

CHAPTER 1

1 F. W. Boreham, *Life Verses: The Bible's Impact on Famous Lives, Vol. Two* (Grand Rapids, MI: Kregel Publications, 1994), 114–115.

2 Tim Kimmel, quoted in Stu Weber, *Tender Warrior* (Sisters, Oreg.: Multnomah Books, 1993), excerpted as "Changed Lives," in *A 4th Course of Chicken Soup for the Soul* (Deerfield, Fla.: Health Communications, 1997), 60–61.

3 Maxie Dunnam, *This Is Christianity* (Nashville: Abingdon Press, 1994), 60–61.

CHAPTER 2

1 Thanks to Landon Saunders for sharing this story with me.

2 Ernest Gordon, *To End All Wars: A True Story About the Will to Survive and the Courage to Forgive* (Grand Rapids: Zondervan, 2002), 105–6, 101.

3 M. Norvel Young with Mary Hollingsworth, *Living Lights, Shining Stars: Ten Secrets to Becoming the Light of the World* (West Monroe, LA: Howard Publishing, 1997), 11–12.

4 "The Candy Bomber," http://www.konnections.com/airlift/candy.htm.

5 Rick Reilly, "The Play of the Year," *Sports Illustrated*, 18 November 2002.

CHAPTER 3

1 Jack Canfield and Mark Hansen, *Chicken Soup for the Soul* (Deerfield Beach, Fla.: Health Communications, 1993), 273–74.

2 Telephone interview with Jo Anne Lyon, conducted by David Drury, 23 June 2009.

3 Not his real name.

CHAPTER 4

1 "Nicholas Winton, the Power of Good," Gelman Educational Foundation, www.powerofgood. net/story.php, and Patrick D. Odum, "Gratitude That Costs Us Something," *Heartlight*, www. heartlight.org/cgi/simplify.cgi?20090922_gratitude.html.

Chapter 5

1   David Jeremiah, *Acts of Love* (Gresham, Ore.: Vision House Publishing, Inc., 1994), 92.

2   *1041 Sermon Illustrations, Ideas and Expositions*, compiled and edited by A. Gordon Nasby (Grand Rapids, MI: Baker, 1953), 180–81.

3   John Bentley, e-mail message to author. Used by permission.

Chapter 6

1   This story is adapted from the book *A Man for Others* by Patricia Treece.

2   "In Praise of Courage," *Quest*, November 1980, 23.

3   "Miracle on Mount Everest," *Dateline NBC*, June 25, 2006, http://www.msnbc.msn.com/id/13543799.

Chapter 7

1   Aleksandr I. Solzhenitsyn, *The Gulag Archipelago, 1918–1956: An Experiment in Literary Investigation*, trans. Thomas P. Whitney (New York: HarperPerennial, 2007), 309–12.

2   David Aikman, *Great Souls: Six Who Changed the Century* (Nashville: Word Publishing, 1998), 341–42.

3   Story taken from *Encyclopedia of 7700 Illustrations*, by Paul Lee Tan.

4   William C. Frey, *The Dance of Hope: Finding Ourselves in the Rhythm of God's Great Story* (Colorado Springs, CO: WaterBrook Press, 2003), 174.

Chapter 8

1   Dan McCarney, "Courage to Quit," *San Antonio Express News*, 13 July 2000, sec. 4C.

2   Bill Tucker (Speech, Oak Hills Church men's conference, San Antonio, TX, May 3, 2003).

 SOURCES

All of the material in this book was originally published in the following books by Max Lucado. All copyrights to the original works are held by the author, Max Lucado.

The Applause of Heaven . . . . (Nashville: Thomas Nelson, Inc., 1990).

In the Eye of the Storm . . . . (Nashville: Thomas Nelson, Inc., 1991).

He Still Moves Stones . . . . (Nashville: Thomas Nelson, Inc., 1993).

A Gentle Thunder . . . . (Nashville: Thomas Nelson, Inc., 1995).

In the Grip of Grace . . . . (Nashville: Thomas Nelson, Inc., 1996).

Just Like Jesus . . . . (Nashville: Thomas Nelson, Inc., 1998).

When Christ Comes . . . . (Nashville: Thomas Nelson, Inc., 1999).

He Chose the Nails . . . . (Nashville: Thomas Nelson, Inc., 2000).

A Love Worth Giving . . . .(Nashville: Thomas Nelson, Inc., 2002).

And the Angels Were Silent . . . . (Nashville: Thomas Nelson, Inc., 2003).

Next Door Savior . . . .(Nashville: Thomas Nelson, Inc., 2003).

No Wonder They Call Him the Savior . . .(Nashville: Thomas Nelson, Inc., 2003).

Six Hours One Friday . . . .(Nashville: Thomas Nelson, Inc., 2003).

Come Thirsty . . . . (Nashville: Thomas Nelson, Inc., 2004).

Cure for the Common Life . . . .(Nashville: Thomas Nelson, Inc., 2005).

Facing Your Giants . . . . (Nashville: Thomas Nelson, Inc., 2006).

3:16: The Numbers of Hope . . . .(Nashville: Thomas Nelson, Inc., 2007).

Every Day Deserves a Chance . . . . (Nashville: Thomas Nelson, Inc., 2007).

On the Anvil . . . . (Wheaton: Tyndale House Publishers, 1985, 2008).

Cast of Characters . . . . (Nashville: Thomas Nelson, Inc., 2008)

Fearless . . . . (Nashville: Thomas Nelson, Inc., 2009).

Outlive Your Life . . . .(Nashville: Thomas Nelson, Inc., 2010).

MAX LUCADO is a minister who writes and a writer who preaches. He and Denalyn serve the Oak Hills Church in San Antonio, Texas. They have three grown daughters—Jenna, Andrea, and Sara; one son-in-law, Brett; and one sweet—but lazy—golden retriever, Molly.

IF YOU HAVE ENJOYED THIS BOOK
OR IT HAS TOUCHED YOUR LIFE IN SOME WAY,
WE WOULD LOVE TO HEAR FROM YOU.

PLEASE SEND YOUR COMMENTS TO:
HALLMARK BOOK FEEDBACK
P.O. BOX 419034
MAIL DROP 215
KANSAS CITY, MO 64141

OR E-MAIL US AT:
BOOKNOTES@HALLMARK.COM